the runner

Traversing the Road of Life

Sidney Barthwell Jr

dedication

This book is dedicated to my loving Wife, Judy,

to all runners everywhere

and to peace on Earth...

contents

chapter one: beginnings

The sweet smell of exhilaration was omnipresent. The excitement of a moment that sometimes raises the life experience to its highest, most memorable level, had blanketed the crowd of athletes of various dimension like the warm womb of the universal mother of us all. The race was about to begin. The marathon. Twenty-six miles, three-hundred and eighty-five yards. Twenty-six long and grueling miles; a distance not meant to be traversed by men or women on foot, running... five or ten miles, maybe; by graceful quadrupeds such as gazelle or horse, certainly. But man...no way! On foot...absolutely not! And running... you must be crazy!

By car, at sixty miles per hour, the distance could be covered in twenty-six minutes. On foot, the fastest man had covered the distance in two hours and six minutes, averaging less than five minutes a mile. For the majority of the people gathered on this cool, clear morning, just finishing the race would be an accomplishment. To finish running, feeling good as in uninjured and minimal pain and in less than four hours would be a major accomplishment. To be in the kind of physical condition to step up to the starting line, to have completed the months of rigorous training needed to attempt the distance, to have endured countless early morning runs in cold, adverse conditions when bed and mate seemed so inviting, was in itself a major accomplishment. To have the strength of character necessary to even conceive of the idea that one could run twenty-six miles was, standing alone, a psychological achievement. And yet, here they were. Thousands of hearty souls, gathered to partake of the rights of passage in the runner's world and attempt to go the distance in the big race.

It was a cool but clear morning in the midwestern city, still gray as dawn was only beginning to break. The slight northwestern breeze was a welcome addition to the climate, as it would serve to enhance rather than hinder the runners' performance. In short, Mother Nature had cooperated with the race; conditions were perfect as the gun sounded and the race began...

This was the beginning; the start; the first steps in a long journey. The point at which hope springs eternal, where all is well with the world and humankind is at peace with himself. There is no war or starvation, no economic depravation or degradation, no injustice or imprisonment, crime, racism, prejudice or hate. Only good feelings and high expectations. Everyone is your friend and we are all sharing in this glorious adventure together, one step at a time. At this stage in the race, the prudent runner is cautious to control his pace. The problem is not going too slow but rather going too fast. If not careful, one will burn out long before the finish, hit the wall... and die. Pace, rather than speed is the thing. It is key the successful completion of the task at hand; it is central to the successful conclusion of the endeavor; it is of paramount importance. So go slowly, my friend. Enjoy the process; immerse yourself in the experience and enjoy. Let your body take your mind on a free ride, courtesy of a thousand hours of training. No pain here. See the sights, smell the smells, listen to the sounds of life. Appreciate and enjoy your life and your being; this is your moment of moments, when you are at one with the universe and united with the godhead.

The start of the marathon is not unlike the beginning of love; not a love developed and nurtured over a long period of time, a love of a maturing teenager for a parent; not that of a love that is gradually learned. Rather, the onset of the race is as love at first sight; pulse-quickening and exciting. It's fun; it's new; it's breathless anticipation of that next unforeseen vision of your new love; it's like making love for the first time. Gradually, that love grows and matures, as feet turn into yards, and the yards turn into tenths, quarters and half-miles. One learns to appreciate the more far-reaching meaning of love and learns how to respect and nurture the object of one's affection. One learns not to become self-consumed at the risk of losing that cherished new love. One learns that to give is to receive, that to love is to be loved, and that the food of love is respect. Respect the race and you will reap its rewards. Love the road and it will return your love a thousand fold. But cheat the road and you will die a thousand deaths... For the road will not tolerate greed nor sanction selfishness.

The runner negotiates a bend in the road and can see tables and a crowd of people, each with cups in hand providing water to the passing runners. Beyond them, barely visible, is a large rectangular sign marked "1", indicating the one-mile mark in the race. The runner feels good, his stride smooth, his pace strong.

The eastern sky is markedly brighter, turning progressively from a rose hue to yellow as the sunrise grows nearer. Billowy clouds are slowly becoming visible in the morning sky, staccatoed in an otherwise clear sky. A slight breeze blows across the brow of the runner, cooling his not yet sweaty body but not inhibiting his progress. It is a good day. Slowing to receive water, he sips ever so slightly from the paper cup, swallowing carefully in between breaths so as not to choke, then pours the remaining water over his head. Feeling no pain and brimming with confidence, with the sun rising in the eastern sky and the die-hard, equally vigilant spectators shouting words of encouragement, the runner glides gracefully by the one-mile marker.

chapter two: life

From a physical perspective, as the runner began the second mile of the long race, he was barely aware of any strain whatsoever. The hype and excitement of the event continued to dominate the moment, not allowing to even the slightest degree, any hint of laboring from the exertion required in the running. It was as though the runner was floating in some time-warp continuum; there was no sensation of working or straining to achieve the pace which he was maintaining. The running, itself, took on an almost metaphysical quality, ethereal and out-of-body... as though it were someone else doing the running, with a camera mounted on his forehead for his viewing at his leisure.

This was fun! Although many a non-running, non-exercising skeptic would scoff at that notion, to the serious athlete and, particularly to the serious runner, there was and is no finer feeling than the seemingly effortless execution of one's chosen athletic endeavor. This was the pinnacle, the apex of the hours and, perhaps, years of strenuous training; to fly like the eagle; to bound swiftly and gracefully as the deer; this was truly reaching that desired level of athletic and physical contentment not unlike the Buddhist state of nirvana. It was a Zen experience... and he felt wonderful!

And yet, for all his good feelings, he understood that the final chapter had not yet been written regarding the race. In fact, he was barely passed the preface. He had run many races before of varying lengths. Each race was unique, taking on its own characteristics, and exacting its particular price from one's body. In some of the shorter races, those of 5,000 meters or four or five miles, one could start off more quickly and run harder from the onset, knowing that the end was not quite so far. In those type races, one did not fear the pain of exhaustion with the same dread as in the marathon. With these runs, he knew that he could "gut it out" and endure the pain of hard running, understanding that it would be quickly at an end.

Not so, however, in the marathon. If you erred in your pace in this race, if you went out too fast, started too quickly, if you were "sucked in" by the feeling of exhilaration at the start of the race, you took the serious risk of expending your energy reserves long before the race was finished. And then you "hit the wall"; that mythical and yet very real barrier when you could run no longer. Typically, this would happen, if at all, at some point between the fifteen and twenty-mile mark. When this happened, exhaustion would be complete; the body, mind and spirit would be drained of every scintilla of energy and motivation. At this point, it was no longer about "gutting it out"; you had been doing that for the last two miles— the guts were gone! At this point, all you were faced with was the fact that you were totally exhausted – a feeling unlike any you had experienced before – with six, seven, eight or nine miles left to negotiate in the race; a distance equivalent to going from one side of town to the other. And you are walking and aching, aching and walking, getting stiffer by the second, visualizing just how far eight miles is, inch-by- inch, step by step. In the entire realm of athletic endeavor and, perhaps, in life, there is no lower, more agonizing experience. It isn't death, but it's close.

And that, my friends, is why the marathon demands respect. It is a sacred undertaking, not unlike life, itself, which requires a certain amount of understanding, reverence and perspective in order to achieve success. As in a marathon, life is a truly glorious happenstance; a wondrous phenomenon, serious and yet somewhat frivolous, stern and yet gay, prudent yet wonderfully uninhibited. It is restrictive but at the same time liberating; it is abstinence and promiscuity.

Life is the one defining experience that separates us, as humanity, from rocks and automobiles and yet, it is all too often the case that life remains, for most of us, unexamined. Life is unconsciously accepted as the state of being of humankind without any serious consideration given to what it is or why we exist. Of course, many would say simply look to the great religions of the world for an explanation of life. God is life; Jesus Christ was his (or her) son and manifestation on earth, and heaven is the ultimate goal and reason for living. Or, perhaps, it is Buddha who is all-knowing and all-powerful, and we should aspire to Nirvana, that glorious selflessness of the universal whole. Or maybe Allah holds the answer, or Zoroaster, Siddhartha, Confucius, Juju or Zeus. Perhaps, the answer lies in some long since forgotten religious doctrine that had the misfortune of never being written, but only verbal, as was all human communication prior to five or six thousand years ago. Or, perhaps, not at all.

Maybe the meaning of life lies not in religious explanation at all, not in the many philosophic treatises examining the same, be it existential or sophism or epicurean, but simply in the process, itself. Perhaps, the meaning of life was simply in the living...

The richness and glory of life cannot be calculated in dollars and cents, or rupees or dinars or pounds. Life is valuable unto itself. It derives its incalculable wealth from its very existence. As the old cliche so truthfully states: "life is the thing". Nothing, no philosophy or religion, defines our being outside of the fact that we live. Take away life and, truly, humanity is swallowed by the void of nothingness. Not only do we cease to exist, existence ceases to exist. For what is existence other than our feelings and observations. Rene Descartes once uttered and wrote the famous line: "I think therefore I am"; but it could be more compellingly said that I live therefore I think. For without life there are no thoughts.

The meaning of life is to be found in the babbling brook on the clear spring day, as well as on the proverbial mountain top. It exists in the first snow of winter and in the aqua blue waters of the Caribbean Sea. It can be found in the soulful sigh and the intimate caress of the beloved, or in the serenity of being alone in a vast meadow. Life's meaning, however, is not confined to these peaceful, loving images. It lies also in its end; in death and dying. So much sweeter the breath with the knowledge that it is not guaranteed. Deeper the meaning of the touch, the gentle word of care, when contrasted to the finality of the grave. One experiences the meaning of life, that intangible, indefinable knowledge of the essence of life most markedly when peering into the cold, quiet, motionless face of death. 'Tis a consummation devotely to be avoided.

Ahead, the runner, still strong and glowing, could see the crowd of volunteers; gradually growing louder was the sound of music: James Brown's soulful classic "I feel good" emanated from roadside speakers. The runner felt good, "...so good, so good, 'cause I got you...". With a bright, but slightly filtered sun arising brilliantly in the eastern sky, our hero of the moment glided by the two-mile marker.

chapter three: nature

As steps and strides turned into blocks, and the urban landmarks slowly drifted by, the runner, still exhilarated with a runner's high and with adrenalin still flowing, was feeling no pain. As he ran, he looked about him. He noticed with acuity the subtleties of the surroundings, as runners often do, and, in particular, the surprising proliferation of nature in the seemingly harsh, unappealing urban landscape.

Nature, he noted, finds a way to survive and even thrive in the most unlikely settings. The race was being run in an older, Midwestern urban area often referred to by those allegedly knowledgeable, actually shallow commentators as the "rust bucket". This was a densely populated metropolis that in the early part of the nineteenth century had been a boomtown of the "industrial revolution". Many such places existed in the large, sprawling nation. At an earlier time, these cities had been the hope and salvation for many poorer, less fortunate citizens from the rural and agricultural areas of the country. In particular, racial and ethnic minorities who had been the victims of earlier widespread and legally sanctioned oppression, had flocked to these cities seeking the high-paying, unskilled jobs that the heavy industry of the era offered them. It was hard, back-breaking, dirty work but it afforded these people their first opportunity at a middle-class lifestyle; a first opportunity to participate in the ideals and lifestyle for which the nation, rightly or wrongly, was famous. It represented to these economically deprived persons a first opportunity to provide for their families the homes, shelter, clothing and education that were an expected and accepted part of life on the other side of town; that side separated from them by railroad tracks, freeways, religions, racial and ethnic distinctions.

Time, however, waits for no one or, perhaps, time changes things – pick you cliche – and, as technologies advanced, as international trade patterns deviated, allowing the exportation of jobs, the markets for the industry and unskilled labor in these great cities declined, leaving in its wake, older, decaying inner-cities with highly polluted grounds that once held thriving factories. Little attention had been given to the environment during industrial boom-times. Now, largely abandoned by those who profited from the act, these cities were left to suffer the consequences of unrestricted market forces. The scene was bleak.

Yet, in the midst of these bleak surroundings, the runner noticed that nature was, in fact, thriving. Trees, scrubs, bushes, grasses and wildflowers of all dimensions were everywhere. This area, in the heart of the great continent, was, in fact, a temperate-zone jungle; greenery thrived and quickly recaptured areas abandoned, intentionally or otherwise, by society. Compared to the dry, arid regions in the western part of the nation, with its dry rivers and desert, this area was incredibly lush and rich in life. One of the profound benefits of running outdoors was that one was in nature and with nature. In nature in the sense that you were one with all of the elements: the wind, the sun, warmth in summer, cold in winter and, as such, developed a unique appreciation of those elements. The wind was something to be respected, not feared. Rain cooled the body and allowed for more efficient running. The wind, likewise, could cool the body, if in a favorable mood, or could stifle forward progress and render one rigid with frost if feeling rather nasty. Snow padded and cushioned weary feet, while sun warmed the soul. To the astute observer, the "dusty road" became a virtual symphony of sounds and sensations. The virtuoso singing of the many birds, the sounds of the wind blowing through the leaves and around the buildings and even the sounds of traffic had their own unique position in the orchestra, although perhaps relegated to the back row of significance.

Complementing the audio concert was the equally splendid visual cacophony of natural delights. Blue skies and sun were and are of legendary import, needing little explanation or description. Billowy clouds and flowing waters were always a pleasure. Equally interesting, however, were the more subtle sights, such as the old wooden buildings, some occupied while others abandoned, the unique shapes of every individual tree and even the cracks in the sidewalks. Dated manhole covers, partially broken streetlamps, the ubiquitous cell-phone towers, the ever-present brown, black and grey squirrels, old cars with fresh, young faces, shiny, new cars carrying self-absorbed, unhappy spinsters, green grass and black dirt, old bricks, granite boulders, winos and rich folks combined to complete the visual montage, rendering a masterpiece worthy of the finest museum.

But, of course, the runner realized that this was the finest museum. A museum without building, budget or Board of Directors, without masterpieces in storage or censorship policies, always open and always free.

Ahead, upon the crest of a slight incline, the sign marking mile-three came into view. As he strode by, the runner accepted a small cup of water from a pretty girl and smiled gratefully. His thoughts were not of the twenty-three miles yet to be traversed but, rather, of his continued good feelings. Running was, indeed, great fun!

chapter four: love

Entering the realm of the fourth mile was something of a landmark for the runner. The four-mile mark was a familiar distance to him. Many times, in training and in shorter races, he had traversed the distance. He was imminently familiar with both his varying paces and times for the distance. He knew that, in the past, he had covered the distance in relatively fast times, particularly in races; he knew also that many times in training, five miles was the distance that he covered. Five miles in forty minutes...eight minutes per mile; forty-two- fifty...eight-thirty; forty-one...eight-twelve; under forty...you're smokin'. He loved that distance; long enough to feel a true sense of physical accomplishment and yet short enough to run hard, if so moved. It was an "in-between" distance. Five could be an easy run, light and breezy, or more difficult, depending on other factors such as relative conditioning, weather conditions and pace. The runner had experienced both phenomena. When training for the marathon, one gets in such good shape that the five-mile training run becomes a short, easy distance; it requires a lesser degree of mental preparedness the deeper one gets into his training schedule. It is a good barometer of one's conditioning. When out of shape, for whatever reason, five miles can be long and difficult. In its running, thoughts of simply completing the run predominate: Am I going too fast to finish...have I reached the half-way point ... can I see the finishing point ... slow down. However, as one's fitness increases the thought pattern changes; thoughts of goals for the day come to the fore; the running becomes easier, almost routine with the predominate thought being: I feel so good that I must be going too fast! The scenery becomes prettier, the air fresher and the load lighter. And, at the end of the run, always astonishment with the faster time: how did I do that?

As he contemplated the fifth mile, the runner realized that he had, in fact, learned to love the distance. Not in the warm, humanistic, interpersonal sense, but rather in a more ethereal, intellectual way. With that realization, the runner considered the complexities of love, and the many varia-tions and manifestations thereof. He knew that he loved deeply. Life, nature, parents, friends, women, men, wife, sib-lings, the air he breathed, the water he drank...life. Love was, perhaps, the important and prevailing emotion and philos-ophy in his life; for all good things and good feelings were somehow connected to love and loving. The joy of loving, the act of giving ones' self to another, of immersing and connecting the individual being with the soul and essence of another had become a defining indicator of content-ment and happiness. Love defined the beauty of life. The runner had come to understand why all the great and noble religions and philosophies had at their core the idea that love was essential to life. Love embodies all that is good; it embraces and highlights the positive qualities of human-kind; it emphasizes and demands kindness and sharing,

selflessness and consideration, the gentle touch of tolerance, the soft caress of forgiveness. When one loves, one is
loved. Love is the reciprocity of compassion at its highest
level. When one loves, pettiness become trivial, selfishness
becomes irrelevant, wants are transformed into passions,
dollars become sense and I becomes WE. Being in love
is the defining state of being. Love separates humankind
from the pre-morphological soup of inception, it elevates
human existence beyond cells and atoms and guarantees
our continued viability as a universal entity. With love, we
become our best thoughts and exhibit our highest ideals.
Without love, the void becomes reality. So hold her hand,
blow a kiss to the World and let the loving continue...

Amidst the love, between the pleasant thoughts, just
beyond the amorphous and down reality's road, a few yards
yonder lay the five-mile marker. The race continued.

chapter five: death

Normally, for the runner, the transition between miles five and six represented a bit of a barrier. In the galaxy of road racing, the marathon was a completely unique experience. Many of the rules that were gospel to other distances, either only barely applied to the marathon, or applied not at all. On the day of the race, all bets were off. In fact, one never knew what kind of a race one would have until the running occurred. However, one thing that all experienced marathoners were familiar with was barriers, or, in runner's parlance, "the wall". Walls were times or certain distances in the race when one's physical and psychic energy reached a low ebb. For a myriad of different reasons, some more rational than others, at certain times the running was simply more difficult than at other times. The intensity of these barriers varied, usually increasing as the distance into the race increased, but, regardless of intensity, they were guaranteed to happen. Every experienced long-distance runner knew when he was likely to "hit" one of these walls. Every runner knew at what distances to expect these challenges; and every runner had developed, through hundreds or, perhaps, thousands of miles of training, strategies for coping with these obstacles. Successfully overcoming these barriers was key to achieving success in the race.

The sixth mile was one such barrier for the runner. However, the intensity and magnitude of this particular wall was extremely minimal. In fact, on this occasion and in this race, the barrier was practically nonexistent. Several reasons accounted for this: first and foremost, the runner was, even after five miles, still riding the wave of adrenalin and excitement caused by the event. Or, in other words, he was still "geeked"; fired-up, pumped and rarin' to go! He knew that this feeling would stay with him for a bit longer. Reasons tangible and intangible determined how long the feeling would last: his level of conditioning, weather conditions, the terrain, the size of the crowd and the number of runners both in the race and running with him, at roughly the same pace. They provided strength and support and helped the miles evaporate; they helped reduce the monotony of running so many miles. There is nothing finer in a marathon than running an effortless mile; looking up and discovering that the last mile has magically disappeared; that with virtually no effort one has "eased on down the road".

As the runner contemplated barriers and walls, happily avoiding them for the time being, he thought of other barriers and walls in life. And with those thoughts came visions of life's ultimate barrier — death: the last great wall. He thought of the profound impact that the certainty of death has had on human history, theology, philosophy, ideology and spirituality. He thought of how the fear of death had been the motivating factor in the development of so many beliefs; and how those beliefs, rightly or wrongly, had come to be so dominant in society.

Religion, with its enticing promise of immortality, was everywhere. In politics, the various candidates, regardless of party or, frequently, ideology, were always claiming and proclaiming their holy righteousness and faith; their cause was God's cause. Many of the religious multitudes in the country would declare on a daily or, perhaps hourly basis, to whomever was available to hear, whether asked or not, that they were "blessed". The air-waves were jammed with evangelists of all descriptions, alternatively warning of impending damnation or offering, for a few dollars, eternal salvation. And yet, these beliefs were all based on several common factors: the belief in an invisible and unseen (except by those fortunate few) being or entity that was all-powerful and, secondly, the collateral belief in life after death, usually in the company of this unseen being. All one had to do to insure entry was to "accept" the philosophy, believe in the unseen being, read the gospel and don't cause trouble by asking questions. One must not ask, "What street does God live on?" or "Hey, Jesus, can I borrow $10,000.00 to pay off the mortgage? I'll pay you back when I get to Heaven."

These beliefs had their origins in pre-historic times, many thousands of years ago, long before humans understood the forces of nature and their relationship to mathematics, physics, astronomy, biology, zoology, life and, ultimately, death. Religions were convenient substitutions, belief paradigms, which filled a void created by a lack of knowledge and understanding of life and nature. Above all, religions provided a workable alternative to the on-going fear of death. They freed humankind, momentarily, from its inevitable demise. That freedom, however, was invalid because, in spite of the wonderful morals and ethics that accompanied these beliefs, at their foundation was the bogeyman.

Death should be celebrated, not feared. Not because of some immortal after-life and the companionship forever with some God-like personage; not because when you die you will go to heaven, the land of milk and honey. Death should be celebrated because without death, life would have no meaning. Without death, life would be an endless journey to nowhere. Without death, there could be no endings or beginnings but rather, only an infinite, endless road. One would have no destinations, no motivations, no mountains to climb, no valleys to cross; only endless oceans or interstate highways. The inevitability of death highlights and emphasizes the gloriousness and righteousness of life. One should not fear death and long for eternal life but, rather, appreciate the meaning that death gives life. Heaven is on earth, righteousness is now, the Temple is the living universe. The bogeyman is dead. He died with the passing of the ancient myths and the relegation of the fairy tales to nursery school.

The wind had increased in intensity. The runner was now confronting a fairly strong head wind which made for more difficult running. The sun had dipped behind a curtain of gray clouds and the humidity had increased. The runner could smell rain; he hoped that if it came, it would be light and intermittent rather than heavy. A light rain would cool the body and enhance the run; a heavy rain would waterlog his shoes and blur his vision, creating a momentary nuisance. Ahead lay the majestic river for which the city was famous; bands played, the people clapped and shouted words of encouragement. Tables ladened with water and gatorade lined either side of the city street; the runner gratefully accepted a cup of water and glided by the six-mile marker. No walls, no barriers...still feeling good!

chapter six: god

A gentle rain began to fall. The runner was thankful for the coolness that the droplets imparted on his body. His strides were smooth and even, rythmically repetitive and reminiscence of a finely tuned engine. At this stage of the race the course followed the bank of the broad river in the center of the metropolitan area. The course had turned eastward, rendering the gusting west wind a helpful tail wind. For the moment, the running was enhanced as the wind pushed the runner along. He was possessed of a sense of well-being, but was aware of the fact that this could rapidly change.

The running of a marathon or, for that matter, any really long race, involved by the participant a constant monitoring of one's physical state-of-being. It was a constant struggle between the body and the mind, with each alternately dominating. At one moment, the body would feel good and operate effortlessly, freeing the mind to meander aimlessly. At other times, the body would tire and battle the intellect. "Why are you doing this to me?", the body would ask the mind. "We are already in great shape! Wasn't that the point of all of this training to begin with? You will be none the worse off if you stop now. You still have time to complete other worthwhile tasks today." It is at these times that all of the long training runs offered their benefit. Because of those long runs, the runner had faced this mental paradox before and knew how to cope. Because of the many long runs he had completed, he knew that his body was easily capable of continuing; he had faced his own internal demons before and he knew that they would eventually dissipate. All that he had to do was to run through it; to simply keep going. Better thoughts were around the bend. Good thoughts, pleasant thoughts and renewed vigor; all these things were just ahead — so keep going.

Now, in the sixth mile, these thoughts were few and fleeting. The runner was strong, the race was young. The rain had ended as quickly as it had begun and the sun was, once again, shining. The morning had awakened in all of its glory and nature was abounding. The temperature was gradually rising, although the early autumn day promised to be a pleasant one; not too hot and not too humid. Perfect for running long distances.

It was partly cloudy, with large patches of blue sky. The gentle breeze, yet a tail wind, rustled the leaves, only beginning to turn their magnificent autumn colors. It was a wonderful time of the year, one that most folks considered ideal. Beautiful autumn days such as this brought to mind thoughts of supreme beings: of Buddha, of Allah, of God. The runner had often wondered about the existence of God. Was there a God; did he or she really exist? If he did, was he a good God, an uncaring God or, perhaps, a hard and cruel taskmaster? Why did so many people throughout the world have such a fanatical belief in these invisible beings, whatever his or her name or form?

These questions had occurred repeatedly in the mind of the runner. He had read many of the great treatises on religions and philosophies: the Bible, the Holy Koran, works on Hindu and Buddhist philosophy, Taoism, Confucianism and others. He had noted that, with few exceptions, all of the great religions and philosophies of the ages had recurring themes. All emphasized good and moral behavior among and between people as a desired goal in life. All shared the concepts of universal love, kindness, selflessness, sharing and a denial of material wealth and believed these to be manifestations of the highest and noblest of human behaviors. Those who exhibited and perfected these behaviors would be rewarded; those who did not would be punished. The runner agreed fervently and wholeheartedly with these ideals and concepts. He believed in the correctness and value of high moral behavior. He believed devoutly in ethical behavior and he tried to live each day in accordance with those beliefs. These things, he felt, were good and desirable and, if adhered to by all, would result in a better world.

He had found, however, that in many instances, those who professed to believe in these things, particularly in the name of this religion or that, in fact, did not behave in a fashion consistent with their professed beliefs. Often, he found, just the opposite was true. Those same persons, fervent and loudest in their pronouncements of religious zeal, were guilty of the greatest transgressions counter to those religious ideals. The hypocrisy was, to him, starkly apparent and yet largely ignored. Repeatedly, he had observed the preachers and reverends of various congregations taking material advantage of their "flock", wearing expensive suits, driving long, fancy cars while the members of the church remained destitute. Equally disturbing to him were the pseudo-political televangelists espousing to millions via the mass-media ideas that bordered on the racist, militarist and capitalist, contrary to the very teachings that they so vehemently professed to believe; all the while, flashing in bold letters on the bottom of the screen the address and 800 number to call to make your donation, all major credit cards accepted.

Nor, he had found, was this a new or modern phenomenon. History was replete with a consistent, continual barrage of atrocities committed in the name of this religion or that deity. The " Sword of Allah " had cut a bloody path through much of Asia, Africa and Europe. The Holy Roman Empire had dominated much of mediaeval Europe in a ruthless and bloody fashion, complete with Inquisitions, torture and executions by fire of countless thousands. In the so-called "New World", the Roman Church divided up the new continent between European nations through artificial "line[s] of demarcation", ignoring the rights of native peoples and, adding insult to injury, sanctioned the slaughter and enslavement of people of color throughout the world, all in the name of Jesus. The litany of outrages was long and consistent, and yet, these religions were not only alive and well, they were thriving! Despite the advent of mankind's social and intellectual evolution, his scientific advancements, moon-walks, molecular biology, DNA and genetic research, these mystical beliefs endured.

The runner was baffled as he figuratively scratched his head. With all the scientific and intellectual advances that humankind had made, why was there so much stubborn persistence in the belief of invisible, unseen entities to which the entire fate of humanity was tied. To the runner, this was just so much twenty-first century "mumbo-jumbo", not to be believed. What the runner did believe in was the on-going spirituality of humanity. He believed that in every person existed a persona, an inner spirit, a "soul" that was basically good. Through this soul, people could, if willing, develop an aura of warmth and contentment about them-selves, their fellow humans and life; internal contentment and external goodness toward others, life and the universe. This internal spirit, to the runner, represented the godhead; that essence of a supreme being to which we all were con-nected. Not life after death, not Heaven or Nirvana, not Catholicism, Protestantism, not the Baptists, the Litanies, the Bible or the Koran, but, rather, that internal warmth and kindness was what connected Humankind with God.

As the runner approached the seven-mile marker, he noticed that the familiar crowd of volunteers and support-ers were fewer. He realized that he had reached a point in the long run where contact with civilization was thinning. In most marathons, with the exception of, perhaps, New York and Boston, one always encountered a point, a time, a dis-tance when the initial excitement and enthusiasm subsided somewhat. There were people and supporters present, only fewer and not quite so loud. It was a reflection of the fact that the volunteers were doing a marathon of their own. They had been out for over an hour, handing out water and encouragement and they were tiring as well. The run-ner realized that he had reached the mid-race phase. Here one fought monotony and attempted to divert the mind from the tendency to count the miles to the finish; it was a daunting task. Break the race up into smaller, manageable segments. As he passed the seven-mile marker, the runner focused only on the next mile: Mile Seven. All was well...

chapter seven: sex

In completing the sixth mile, the runner was beginning to feel as though he had finally achieved marathon status. The heart of the race lay ahead. It was time to crunch out a few miles, to maintain a smooth, steady pace, to run easy, enjoy the scenery and flow to the half-way mark, seven miles down the road. The day had blossomed into a wonderful combination of nature's beauty. Blue sky, gentle breeze, partly sunny — warming the spirit without overheating the body. The temperature, the runner guessed, was in the mid-50's, ideal for the long run.

The runner had fallen in pace with a moderate size pack of runners, all running at about the same pace. This was comforting. In a marathon, particularly one of moderate or larger size, with a minimum of two or three thousand runners, one was constantly in the company of other runners. Often, actually almost always, at various segments during the race, a runner would find him or herself running with many of the same runners. One would notice their clothing, the t-shirts or other tops, the writings or colors on their clothing which often identified other races or marathons in which they had run, their names or cities of origin. Frequently, conversations, usually brief in duration, would strike up, with the runners talking idle "running talk": "what pace are we running?... what was the last mile-marker?...how do you feel?". The companionship and support of running with somebody helped runners through the grind of negotiating the continuous miles of the marathon. It made the race easier.

Often, these instantaneous relationship would end as quickly as they had begun. Pace dictated everything. To the savvy, experienced marathoner, even a pace ten or fifteen seconds per mile faster than his or her intended pace was noticeable. The inherent danger of running with others in the race, or joining the "pack" was that often the pace would be slightly faster than the runner's desired pace. It was difficult to notice this subtle difference initially; the thrill of the race or overconfidence were often the dominant factors in these situations. The desire to have a running companion, along with the fact that initially one barely noticed the change of pace also contributed to the phenomena. If one fell into this trap, one would surely pay a price later in the race. That price was a severe one; slowly fading and "dying" in the later segments of the race. Perhaps, even (perish the thought) walking, a fate worse than death! The prudent runner, despite feeling good and enjoying the company, would quickly recognize the quicker pace and allow the faster runners to drift ahead. Invariably, this prudent runner was rewarded later in the race when many of the quicker-paced runners would fade. At that point in the race, usually between the twenty-mile mark and the finish, our prudent runner would pass many of the early jackrabbits, who would be either barely running or walking. They represented the inexperienced marathoners. They had made the cardinal error of "going out" too fast, an easy mistake to make. In their early enthusiasm, they had not held back, they had not monitored carefully their pace, they had allowed the pack of runners to pull them along, with their sirens' song, only to fade — to "die" in the later miles. In marathoning, there is no worse feeling than "dying". It happens subtlety at first; one is running along smoothly, at the desired pace when you notice that you are slowing ever so slightly. This slowing quickly becomes more acute and, at this point, the dye is cast. No matter what sort of strategies the runner tries to counteract the inevitable (slowing the pace dramatically is the usual), eventually the runner will end up walking. This experience is extremely disheartening for it represents defeat to the runner. All that he has trained for, the early mornings and long miles, seem to be for naught, as he walks that first step. Fifteen, seventeen or nineteen miles into the race, it matters not; start walking and you still have eleven, nine or seven miles to go. Projected times go out the window and visions of running a strong race dissipate with each walked step. What a bummer!

As the runner glided along, holding his pace and feeling good, he thought about how profound and positive the impact of running had been on his life. In the earlier phase of his life, the runner had not, at all, been a runner. His life, among other things, had been given to drink, smoke and other unnatural and unhealthy habits. Although his mind had been sound and his intellect vibrant, his body had been a wreak; out of shape, out of condition and deteriorating rapidly. In fact, at age thirty-five, although there were no acute symptoms, he knew that he was slowly dying and was headed for a prematurely early death. His head often ached with severe hangovers, his back ached, his abdomen was in constant pain and he had that hacking smoker's cough. He suffered from high blood pressure, shortness of breath and was in constant fear of heart attack. And to make matters worse, he also suffered from intermittent impotence.

At that point in his life, however, at its darkest moment, the desire for a meaningful, longer life had overcome his earlier transgressions. He had managed to vanquish himself of his bad habits, particularly drinking and smoking, and had gradually started running. Initially combining running with walking, his lungs had, at first, burned in their objection to his newly found lifestyle. Quickly, however, the benefits of running exhibited themselves. Almost immediately, he began to feel physically better; after the initial stiffness, his body began to feel really good for the first time in years. The pains and aches quickly receded and his lungs began to open up; he could breath deeply again and he loved it. He was reintroduced to the beauty of life through the wonders and glories of a healthy body. And, perhaps, best of all, all vestiges of impotency disappeared. His sexuality returned in all it erect glory. He learned through experience the direct connection between exercise and vitality.

The renaissance of vitality in the runner's life had a deep and enduring impact of his sense of well-being. The importance and significance of sex on life and society was not a newly found idea; it was, in fact, as old as history. The history of humankind was the history of sex. Sex was, periodically, devil or angel, sinful or savior, bad or good, evil or wonderfully necessary. Obviously, sex was necessary for reproduction and the perpetuation of the species. Sex, however, and the phenomena that accompanied the idea of sex was much greater than the simple act of intercourse. Sex was an indispensible component of interpersonal relationships and, in following, Love. Although there were many who would claim that sex was unnecessary for the true love between a man and a woman or, for that matter, in same-sex relationships, this was a philosophy to which the runner did not subscribe. He believed that, in fact, good and active sexual relations between people, between a man and a woman or a husband and wife, was the glue that secured the relationship. Good sex made people feel good; good about the impending day, good about life and, significantly, good about each other. A positive sexual experience made people more tolerance toward one another, less likely to see fault in the other person and, when that fault was observed, more likely not to comment. Sex made people glow and smile; it made a bad day tolerable and a good day great. It was fun and enjoyable and enhanced life to the highest degree. It made one feel youthful, vital and alive. It was a good thing!

As the runner approach the eight-mile marker, he smiled. It was a smile of satisfaction and good feeling. He knew that life was good and that all was well. The first seven miles had, indeed, gone well. Ahead, mile eight...

chapter eight: friendship

In the running of countless training runs, as well as his several marathons, the runner had found that mile nine was always a particular challenge. When into the ninth mile, one was no longer in the beginning of the race. Any feelings of enthusiasm that one had at the start of the race had now evolved into a more even-tempered determination. Now the runner had progressed into a mid-race psyche; run evenly, watch your pace, continue to feel good. This was the time to double check your shoes, to be certain that no foot problems that could render the race either impossible or much more difficult occurred. Were your feet comfortable? Did your toes have enough room? How did the corn on your right baby-toe feel? Any tell-tail signs of blisters? In a long run, if these things were going to happen, they usually started by the eight or nine mile mark. The longer that you ran pain and problem free, the more likely that you would complete the race problem free. So far, the runner was, in fact, problem free. This was good; one less thing to worry about. It was always interesting to the runner how various running-related problems were important and occupied conscious space only if they occurred. Otherwise, it was out-of-sight, out-of-mind.

The course had turned inland from the river and was now traversing an older, ethnic neighborhood of the city. Although the spectators along the course were fewer, those who were out this morning were verbose and energetic. This particular section of town was predominantly Hispanic; bands were playing and people were even dancing on the side of the wide boulevard. The area was densely populated, with three, four and five-story apartment buildings lining the street. These buildings served as an effective wind blockade, which was beneficial to the runners. Always, in urban marathons that actually went through the cities, rather than those artificial lay-outs that avoided the poorer sections of town, the runner had always found it intensely interesting to observe the human condition in these sections of the cities. Usually, along with the expected standard civic fluff exhibited for the runners, there was an assortment of denizens of the city to be seen. Homeless persons, hustlers, the occasional prostitute attempting to catch an early morning trick; the neighborhood people who were either oblivious to the strangers running down their block or were pleasantly surprised at the unusual attention their often ignored neighborhood was getting. The young boys who were clad only in undergarments, their heads still groggy from the last evening's activities. The old men who sat on the stoops and sidewalks watching the runners and the world go by, possessing the wisdom of the ages but little else. And always, those few impatient individuals whose only desire was to cross the street ("those damn runners!"), who occasionally darted out in front of the runners, invariably causing a few strides to be broken. Although the runner was aware of the fact that many suburban runners disliked these type of courses, he loved them. To him, this was the epitome of urban road running; experiencing the richness and diversity of the cityscape as a moving vehicle, just passing through. Running was more than just exercise; it was more than just a competition or a task to be completed. Running was a metaphysical, transcendental, existential experience; it was a merging of the being with nature, a confluence of the soul with life. It was to be experienced and, as such, suffered when it was confined to only beautiful parks and scenic country roads. Life was everywhere, thought the runner, so to should be the running.

Thoughts of running and life led the runner to thoughts of people and relationships. Not of past or present loves, as sweet as those thoughts could be, but rather of friends; of those precious relationships remembered and experienced, of long or, perhaps, not so long endurance, the recollection of which brought joy to one's heart and warmth to the spirit. The runner had always prided himself on his ability to make and keep friends. To him, it was an art form; taken lightly by some but an art form, nonetheless. For him, friends had been his security blanket; his protection against an often "cold and seasonless world" of perpetual north winds. He had found endless hours of joy and comfort not only in the company of his many friends, but also in the knowledge of their existence and in the memories of good times had. In particular, he had the good fortune to have maintained several almost lifelong friendships. Friendships that were conceived in grammar school or before and had continued to his present age of almost fifty years. As the years had gently and gloriously drifted by, these long-term friendships had achieved greater meaning and significance. Their endurance alone had made them special. There was a wonderful recognition on the part of both parties that relationships such as these were of a growing heightened importance. These relationships were the living manifestation of a true love between beings; they were great! Sadly, the runner thought of those unfortunate souls who had, through some misdirected twist of fate, not experienced these wonderful, long term friendships. He had encountered from time to time, people, often bitter and unhappy, who lamented their friendless condition. It was, indeed, a sad commentary of life. Usually, these same persons who cursed the cruel destiny that had left them friendless were also persons whose perspective and visions of life were internally directed. They were vain, self-centered individuals, with an emphasis on the "I", who had fail to learn the basis construct of relationships which decreed that giving, selflessness and sharing were at the center of all successful human relationships. It was the destiny of the greedy to be lonely.

As the marathon wound its way through the city streets, the runner was acutely aware of the varying surfaces upon which he and the thousands of fellow runners were treading. In most American cities, the majority of the streets were usually paved with asphalt, the black bituminous material so popular in modern road building. Asphalt, although of questionable credibility and durability as a road surface for heavy automobile traffic, was a very good surface for running. It was soft and forgiving, particularly when relatively new, not unlike the surfaces on all-weather tracks.

As it grew older, however, it became compressed from the weight of the thousands of cars using the road and, as a result, became harder and less forgiving, on cars and runners alike. Nonetheless, asphalt was preferable to most of the alternatives. Some cities, particularly in southern climes where severe (i.e., cold) weather was not a problem, concrete was the road building surface of choice. Some of the older eastern cities even had some roads of brick or cobblestone. All of these surfaces were dreaded by runners; they were super-hard and caused extreme shock to the body. In those runners who had knee, joint or shin problems, these surfaces were practically impossible to endure for any significant distance. Even for more durable runners, the harder surfaces made the longer races much more difficult. For the marathon distance, no race director in his right mind would design a race with more the a few miles of those harder surfaces; the criticism from the running community would be relentless. Consequently, in most marathons, the majority of miles were run on these softer surfaces.

Once again the wind was freshening; the leaves on the stately oak trees that lined the street on this section of the course, rustled gently. The billowy clouds had momentarily blotted out the sun, giving the runner a natural, air-conditioned respite from the sun's now bright intensely. Just ahead, amidst the crowd, water tables and music, was the nine-mile sign. Momentarily awakened from the semi-consciousness of introspection, the runner, water in hand, continued on his journey.

chapter nine: race

The clouds that earlier had provided much needed shade from the rays of the sun, suddenly had become the purveyors of fierce downpour. The large and driving raindrops, along with an accompanying stiff wind, served to drop the perception that the runner had of the temperature significantly. It was now very cool. The short-sleeved t-shirt that had been the perfect garment only moments earlier, now provided little protection for the runner. Silently, he cursed the fates that had brought such a hard and driving rain. Usually, during a marathon, the participants relished a cooling rain; the moisture served to assist the body in the essential cooling process, necessary to ensure a long and successful run. Under normal circumstances, warmth rather than coolness was the enemy of the long distance runner. It was heat and humidity that rendered runners more easily exhausted and hastened the arrival of the dreaded wall. Contrary to the perceptions of normal, lay persons, the non-runners of the world, sunny and eighty-five degrees was not a beautiful day to the runner; not until after the race. Perfection was the mid to upper fifties and partly cloudy. At that temperature the body functioned best while exerting and maintaining a maximum physical effort. Variations from those ideal conditions affected different runners in different ways, dependent on a number of factors. These factors included the conditions under which the runner was accustomed to training in, the experience of the runner in recognizing and adjusting to different conditions and in which conditions the runner was most comfortable.

The runner had noticed also that the racial and ethnic background of the runner had an impact on which running conditions were preferable: African and African-American runners, along with other runners of color, seemed to prefer warmer conditions and tolerated heat better than European and other Caucasian runners, who seemed to like the cooler days better, and wore fewer and lighter clothing while running. He had noticed also that runners whose lineage was from the warmer regions of the world needed less water during these long runs. All of the current running literature and periodicals, when addressing the question of hydration in marathons, always suggested that runners drink water at every water station during the race, which usually occurred every mile. The runner had found through experience that this was, in fact, too much water for him. In his conversations with other runners of color, he had found that their experiences had been similar. This had led the runner to the conclusion that this running literature, probably unbeknownst to the author, had been written for and from the perspective of a white runner only. This form of unconscious, non-malicious racially bias behavior was common in the great nation. The runner, himself a person of color, had been aware of this great issue in the country since early childhood. He remembered as a child listening to the debates that his parents and other relatives had engaged in at various family gatherings. Always, the issue of the plight of "his people" and their discriminatory and unjust treatment at the hands of the white majority of the nation had been a hot topic of conversation. The runner, as a young person, was slow to learn to the full meaning of these issues. He had noticed at the elementary school he attended that the students had changed from predominantly white to predominantly Black during his six years at the school. As he grew older, he had learned that the law of the land included mandating separate toilets and water fountains for black people, that black people lived in a separate part of the city, were not allowed in the more exclusive clubs and organizations of the liberal and "racially tolerant" city and, in many regions of the nation, were relegated to the back of the bus when riding public transportation. He had often wondered why these anonymous white people that he saw on television with their water hoses and police dogs so hated Black people and why the racial animus directed at his people was so pervasive in the great nation.

As the runner had matured, so had the nation. A great civil rights movement had swept across the nation and the people had demanded an end to the discriminatory laws and practices. As a result of this movement, the racially bias laws had been gradually abolished and the discrimination sanctioned by them outlawed. However, the residual affects of four-hundred and fifty years of slavery, racism and discrimination did not disappear overnight. In fact, in the runner's mind, the more difficult battle lay ahead. The battle now was being fought not against overtly discriminatory practices and laws and outrageous racists and bigots, but rather the battlefront had moved to the hearts and minds of the people. The enemy of racial justice and fair play was now embedded in the unconscious minds of the majority race, manifested through the tens of thousands of decisions made every day by white people that affected the lives of people of color. This was the silent enemy of cultural racism; an enemy which in the minds of those most guilty of perpetuating this malady, did not exist.

That people of color and various other ethnic and racial minorities continued to be denied economic parity in the great nation was undeniable. Great ghettos of poverty continued to exist in the inner cities around the country. Native Americans, despite the apparent new-found wealth of casinos, continued to suffer from a host of negative conditions on the various reservations around the country. Every economic survey continued to show a wide gap between the average income of white people and people of color, despite improvements in the size of the Black middle-class. And, perhaps most telling, the life expectancy and infant mortality rate among Black people were, respectively, much shorter and much greater than comparable figures concerning white people. Black folks were leaving sweet life with both a greater frequency at its beginning and much earlier at its end, a truly sad state of affairs. Yet, incredibly, it appear that to the majority of white persons in the great nation, no problem existed. Of course, all persons in the nation acknowledged that things were, perhaps, not quite as good for minorities and others as they were for the majority, but that acknowledgement was increasingly made on a conditional basis: "... things were not as good, but they weren't bad either...African-Americans and others needed to quit crying in their soup; after all, they were far better off than those people in Africa, Asia and South America....".

The perspective of the African-American and other peoples of color in the great nation was far different. Racial issues, and in particular, issues of justice, equal opportunity, civil liberties and racially respectful treatment were of the highest important in the minority family and community. They were issues that were omnipresent in the minds and hearts of people of color. Being the historic victims of societal oppression, African-Americans bore the scar of psychological oppression as well. It translated into behaviors inculcated into the African-American subculture, subtle and often covert, that made complete assimilation into Anglo-American society virtually impossible. The burden of this history was something that every African-American man, woman and child carried within themselves from the cradle to the grave. It was, indeed, a heavy burden: the Black man's burden.

Excitement was building in the runner's consciousness. Despite his best efforts, his pace quickened; the tingling sensation in his body was building. All that had proceeded was mere warm-up, child's play; stuff that any rank amateur could handle. Behind was week-end jogger's territory; ahead lay the real test. The real race was about to begin; double figures, serious miles. Ahead, amidst much fanfare, noise and celebration: the ten-mile mark.

chapter ten: politics

Inch by inch, foot by foot, step by step, the runner neared ever closer to the finish of the great race. But this was, once again, getting dangerously ahead of one's self. Stay focused on now; keep your goals immediate and localized. Zero in on the nearby landmarks — a tree or lamp-post in the not so distant future, just down the road a bit. Focus on the runners near you; what does the shirt immediately in front of you say? Do you know that race; have you been to that locale? How do your fellow runners look? How tall is that fellow just ahead? Are the female runners attractive? Do they look strong in their strides; of course, they do. For some reason, the other runners always looked strong. That is because they have trained so much harder and better than you. Everyone that you see is in better shape than are you. They are all great runners, of outstanding endurance while you are only a pretender; a 10-K runner trying to go marathon distance. The road will surely collect it inevitable toll.

Focus! The runner's mind was drifting, as it is prone to in the middle of a long run. Working on mile eleven was clearly in mid-race. One's body was now functioning with machine-like efficiency. Gone were the early race jitters. Vanquished were all thoughts of conditioning uncertainty; they had been replaced with firm, recent remembrances of one's feelings during the middle of the many long training runs that had been completed. Now, a certain feeling of confidence and efficacy predominated. At this juncture, the runner knew that he was in the requisite shape to run strong for the next few miles at least. In fact, now, at mid-race, the runner knew that he was in marathon condition regardless of what might happen down the road. He was feeling good because his body was telling him that he had done his homework. It was saying "jump on for the ride, mind, I'll take care of you!". At these times in the race, when feelings of confidence abounded, runners hit a groove. It was a time when the road simply flowed under one's feet. Glancing to the left or right, one saw the scenery gently gliding by as though one was riding by in a slow car or coasting on a bicycle. It was a almost surrealistic, with a dream-like quality as though these things were happening to someone else and you were simply an observer. But the miles were slowly passing by, the distance to the finish was steadily decreasing and the distance traversed was becoming increasingly impressive. This was real. Runners invariably loved these times in the race. They were the reward for all of the long, hard training. They were the moment, mistakenly thought frequent by non-runners but, in reality, exceedingly rare, when the running was actually easy and even pleasurable. This was bonus time! Ride that wave to its full extent; the hills were coming.

During this momentary respite, this break in the agony of the miles, the runner's mind once again drifted. The race had turned into an intermittently commercial and residential section of the city. On some of the buildings, in the windows of the small shops and on some of the old wooden utility poles, the runner began to see political campaign signs. "Jones for Judge...Miller for Mayor...Robinson for Council"; some faded, indicative of long past campaigns, some new and fresh, signaling impending elections. In the great nation, the political system was an electoral one, a representative democracy in which the eligible voters elected representatives to govern the city, the state and the country. It was a system much bally-hoed by its success-ful participants. Those elected to office praised the system loudly and frequently. Those whose careers were indelibly tied to the political system, were likewise very vocally sup-portive of the system. Media-types wrote volumes, praising the justness and worthiness of the system, commentators and tele-journalists trumpeted the superiority of the sys-tem, while belittling and deriding other political systems, in theory and in practice, in other parts of the world. This was, as folks liked to say, the "land of the free and the home of the brave." Yet, the runner, himself a student of history and politics and an occasional participant in the internal poli-tics of the city and the nation, knew that a deeper analysis revealed certain flaws in the system. The system was one based on a capitalist economic theory and a democratic political system; a democratic-capitalistic system. In much of the political commentary of the day, these two concepts were often used interchangeably, implying that one could not exist without the other. The runner, through his study of political systems throughout the world, knew this to be a false implication. Many of the European nations, in fact, had very successful social-democratic regimes, with an economic system based more on a blend of socialistic and capitalistic ideas. In these systems, the government, to varying degrees, took responsibility for guaranteeing basic social services for the nation's population. All of these nations, for example, had some form of nationalized health-care systems, leaving no citizen without basic health-care services. The poorer citizens of these countries were also provided with basic food, shelter and clothing. In this great nation, however, although it was the most prosperous country in the world, these things were not provided for the economically deprived citizens of the country. There was an attitude in the country that those who had less, or nothing at all, were themselves wholly to blame for their plight and should be made to suffer the consequences. As a result of this unenlightened policy, tens of millions of persons in the great nation were without basic health-care, millions of people in the great nation were homeless and the jails were overflowing with inmates incarcerated for solely economic crimes, based on their impoverished condition. Conversely, while this economic misery existed unchecked in the central cities and rural farmlands, the upper and middle classes of the great nation were experiencing an unparalleled period of prosperity. The gap between the rich and the poor in the great nation had never been greater. It seemed to the runner that the people of the country had become increasingly cold and uncompassionate to the condition of their fellow man. This greatly sadden the runner, for he loved the great nation and the wonderful ideals that its founders had enunciated: "We hold these truths to be self-evident that all men are created equal; that they are endowed by their creator with certain unalienable rights; that among these rights are life, liberty and the pursuit of happiness...". These high principles expressed by these early leaders of the great nation were, perhaps, the purest expressions of political morality and humanity ever written. Sadly, the input and meaning of those noble words had somehow been lost over time. Although, at election time, on civic holidays and the like, lip service was paid to these ideals, and all of the many speakers swore allegiance to the same, the spirit of the ideals of the early leaders had faded in an avalanche of greed and avarice.

The great nation had, in fact, become a nation governed by an oligarchy of powerful and wealthy special interests. Elections were financed by well-heeled special interest groups and wealthy individuals. Their outcomes were determined through expensive campaigns dominated by sophisticated mass-media strategies affordable only to those fortune few candidates and incumbents backed by these wealthy entities. The ordinary citizen, although civic-minded and energetic, unless able to persuade a well-endowed patron to back his or her campaign, had no chance of election. Once in office, elected officials traded support for contributions to perpetuate their stay in office, rendering impossible the passage of legislation to end this insidious cycle. To the contrary, the influence of these powerful interests was feeding upon the system and growing, as its advocates had become increasing emboldened by their successes. It was, indeed, a vicious cycle, empowering the wealthy, and particularly the corporate sector, at the expense of the ordinary citizen. Particularly disheartening to the runner was the fact that the vast majority of those disempowered citizens, through a sophisticated media campaign financed by those same wealthy interest groups, were unaware of their own political manipulation. Ignorance was bliss. Particularly when the beer was plentiful and the cars were new.

As he gazed above at the somewhat overcast sky and felt the breeze against his face, he noticed that for the first time in quite a while, there were no runners in his immediate vicinity. He could look to his right or left and see only the side of the road going by. Ahead, the pack of runners were at least twenty yards in front of him. Behind —- who knows? He could not hear the familiar noise of runners to his rear, footsteps or occasional conversation, but he almost never looked to the rear. An old principle of track training was to never look behind; the runner had learned that years ago when he was a high school athlete. The lesson had stuck. Not only did he not look behind, he did not even consider looking behind. The race was too long, there were too many miles to go to be concerned about what was behind. Ahead was the thing. Onward to the finish!

Ahead, once again, was the familiar hub-bub of folks gathered at the mile marker. Water, gatorade, vasoline in large globs and sections of fruits were, as usual, being offered by the hardy volunteers. Words of encouragement greeted the steadfast and determined athletes. A large digital display on the side of the road flashed the elapsed time to the runners. One of the volunteers, decked out in his running regalia to show that he was a member in good standing of the runner's fraternity, barked out the times as the people passed: "one-twenty-eight-ten...one-twenty-eight-twenty". One hour, twenty-eight minutes and twenty seconds, thought the runner; quickly calculating in his head. That translated into an eight minutes per mile pace, or a three hour, twenty-nine minute marathon. Good, he surmised, approvingly. That would be a decent time. As the eleven-mile mark passed, he thought for only the briefest of moments, fifteen miles to go...

chapter eleven: law

Passing the eleven-mile sign, the runner, as usual, immediately began thinking in terms of running "the twelfth
mile:. He did not think in terms of a percentage of the eleventh mile, although that would have been the more accurate distance, but rather, he thought: "I'm into the twelfth
mile...".These kinds of mind games occurred with great frequency during the running of a marathon. The problem, as
it were, was that one had to develop strategies to neutralize
negative thoughts during the long run. The body might be
willing but the mind would often resist the idea of running
twenty-six miles; particularly in the middle of the race, when
one had already run a considerable distance but had a long
way to go. One of the benefits of training with long runs of
fifteen to twenty miles was that in addition to getting the
body into shape, the runner was getting his mind into shape
as well. One was adjusting and adapting mentally to the
idea of running non-stop for three or four hours. One was
toughening one's psyche to deal with the sheer monotony
and boredom of simply running for so long a period. This
was no small task. Very infrequently in life was one called
upon to do anything for four hours straight. At the job, workers routinely received breaks after two hours. In school or at
the university, classes rarely lasted longer than one-hour

without a break. And these were fairly non-intensive activities. Running, on the other hand, was an extremely intense physical activity, described by the sports physiologists as "vigorous exercise". No other athletic endeavor demanded the sustained, long-term effort of long-distance running. Football and baseball involved mostly standing around with occasional spurts of activity. Both included in their make-up periods when the players would sit and rest, either while batting in baseball or in the transition between offense and defense in football. Basketball and soccer required more running but with varying levels of intensity. In basketball, one changed speeds often and there were frequent stoppages of play for various reasons (time-outs, free-throws, half-time, etc.). In soccer, the field was large, with many players on each side, allowing for ample rest when the ball was not in one's immediate area. In either case, the games lasted only forty-eight minutes in basketball (pro basketball; games are shorter in college and high school) and two halves of forty-five minutes in soccer. By contrast, running a marathon required, for the average participant, three to five hours of steady, uninterrupted, competitive running, presumably, as fast as you can go given the distance.

This was a unique athletic experience requiring great mental discipline. The mind, undisciplined and untrained, was the declared enemy of the potential marathon runner. It would rationalize away one's race almost before it began. One's reasoning would attack the premise of running so far; the pain and sensation centers in the brain would sent out signals of agony, aches and pains, imploring the runner to come to his or her senses and stop this madness. This thought pattern would eventually weaken one's resolve and win, so to speak, the day, causing the runner to start walking or worse, drop out of the race. The highly disciplined mind, on the other hand, learned to overcome such negative thoughts and replace them with positive images. Aches and pains became signs that the body was functioning efficiently and became acceptable. Thoughts of stopping were replaced with thoughts of the excitement of the finish. Instead of agonizing over the length of the race, instead of deliberating over the number of miles to the finish, one learned to appreciate, in mid-race, the many positive benefits of being in great shape and set immediate short goals in the running process. One thought of the next mile or two, rather than the ten or twelve to the finish. One thought in terms of small segments, little goals: the next ten minutes, a nearby, visible land-mark, the top of the next hill, the next three traffic lights and the like. And one counted; steps, every fourth step, breaths, up to hundred and back, or a thousand, or more. Anything to help the miles melt away.

The more that one trained and practiced, the more experience that one had running marathons, the better one became at overcoming these mental obstacles. The runner had completed dozens of marathons and hundreds of other races. In the process, he had become adept at controlling these mental processes most of the time. No one, no matter how experienced, was totally free of these mental demons, but their presence was greatly diminished by the presence of the "white knights" of confidence and experience. With these gallant saviors along for the ride, the race became, for increasingly greater periods, less tedious and tiresome, and even enjoyable.

In the highly valued company of these trusted companions, the runner forged ahead. Not into the eleventh plus mile, but rather, for all of the right reasons, into the twelfth mile. He was feeling good! As the runner progressed, the course took him past a fairly large thoroughfare. Traffic on the eight-lane street, although fairly light on Sunday morning, was somewhat backed up, waiting for the clusters of runners. On either side of the runners, smartly dressed police officers, decked out in shiny leather knee boots and white gloves, were directing traffic. Even an impatient look for the anxious drivers would elicit a stern response from the officers, intent on doing their duty. The runner was grateful for the protection that the officers provided the runners from the cars. On one occasion, in the amidst of a training run, he had been hit by a careless driver. Cars were a constant danger to road runners, with many a good runner having been crippled or killed by wayward drivers. Often the runners were, themselves, responsible for these accidents, forgetting that at dawn or dust, in the twilight, runners were invisible to drivers and carelessly taking unnecessary risks.

On this occasion, however, the presence of the police officers stimulated thoughts on the part of the runner of the law. The runner had always been intensely interested in the law in all aspects. His interest, in fact, had eventually led him to law school for a deeper study of law and, afterwards, to a career as an attorney. He had been initially attracted to the law due to the impact of the law on the condition of his people. As a younger person, it seemed to him that the letter of the law and its enforcement or lack thereof, was indelibly tied to the freedom or oppression of people in society. During the height of the civil rights movement of the African-Americans, the passage and interpretation of various laws and constitutional amendments, as well as the repeal, rescission and overturning of other laws and legal principles, was key to obtaining certain rights and liberties for African-Americans and , for that matter, all other Americans. The runner had been acutely aware of the fact that when all other resources had appeared to fail, various judicial decisions had been the key in securing redress from the old oppressive laws. The Courts, it had seemed, were the only branch of government that Black people could look to with the hope of obtaining relief from the brutal and unjust laws of segregation and discrimination. These decisions and their impact on society had made a deep and lasting impression on the runner as a young person, and had served to influence him, in later years, to pursue law as a career. However, as he had learned more about the actual functioning of the law in society, the runner had lost some of his youthful enthusiasm and idealism, to be replaced by a more pragmatic assessment of the law.

Historically, laws had developed out of the societal necessity for rules of behavior among people. In ancient times, men and societies had developed codes and laws, both in the civil and religious arena that contained in their essence the high moral ideals of the times. These codes, such as Hammurabi's Code and the Ten Commandments, were designed with the underlying idea that they would codify justice and morality and, in doing so, make society a better place to live. The law would prevent the random injustices and abuses of powerful sovereigns and, also, regulate the business relationships between traders and merchants, preventing theft, cheating and larceny. Laws also served the purpose of attempting to decrease assaultive and murderous behavior among men by providing for uniform punishments for such acts. The essence and foundation, history and original purpose of the law was to establish a standard of moral behavior in society that would promote and enhance compassion, humanity and harmony in society.

From these pure and humble beginnings, however, the law and the enforcement and punishment associated with those laws evolved into many things, often losing connection with its noble beginnings. Societies, and the men (and sometimes women) controlling them, began to modify and structure laws to promote their own purposes. Often, these purposes had little or nothing to do with the bettering of society but were merely devices utilized to enhance the power and wealth of these rulers or leaders. The lesson of history regarding the law and laws, generally, is that laws are only as good as those creating and enforcing them. When the leaders are wise and of noble character, the laws are reflective of wisdom and nobility. When the leaders are vain and corrupt, the laws become the tool of a corrupt society, oppressive and unjust.

In the great nation in which he lived, the laws had been, at different times in the history of the country, both good and just and oppressive and unjust. In fact, at any given time in the country, because of the immense size of the country and the proclivity the nation had for producing so many laws, there were always both good - as in just - and bad – as in unjust – laws in effect. Because there were so many jurisdictions in the great nation — the national government, states, counties, commonwealths, parishes, cities, villages and townships — all of which had legislative bodies that promulgated laws at a breakneck pace, there were literally millions of laws on the books. Millions of laws, hundred of thousands of attorneys and tens of thousands of judges. Local judges, state judges and federal judges. Appellate judges, district judges, probate judges, juvenile judges, common pleas judges, administrative judges, magistrates, referees and, of course, the almighty Supreme Court Judges, otherwise known as Justices. Judges, among other things, interpreted these millions of laws. Judges, in their courtrooms, exercised an inordinate amount of discretionary authority. They were, in effect, the rulers of their small kingdoms; the final word of justice, as it were. Although the law, as it was structured, allowed for appeals of lower court decisions, for the vast majority of cases, regardless of the correctness of the outcome, the first and last word on the case came from the first judge to hear the case. Thus, if one had the misfortune of appearing before a bad judge, a judge who, for whatever reason, had a negative bias against you, a judge who did not know the relevant law involved in the case or worst, didn't care; a judge who was more concerned about his or her own political agenda than about fairness; if, for any of these reasons or a myriad of others, one had the misfortune of appearing before such a judge, that was just your bad luck. The chances of a bad decision being reversed on appeal were exceedingly remote. Most could not afford the high legal fees required for an appeal. In fact, those who were most likely to be mistreated in the lower courts, i.e., poor minorities, were the same persons least likely to appeal.

In the great nation, the application of the laws, the behaviors designated as criminal and the punishments for such crimes had become increasingly harsh. As the politicians had discovered that being "hard on crime" was a relatively easy (and mindless) way to gain votes, the range of behaviors that had been criminalized had become ever wider. And the punishments for violating these increasingly broad laws had become harsher. Of particular popularity was the sanctioning and criminalizing of the use and sale of certain drugs in the culture. The history of drug use in human culture was as old as history itself. Drug use, from ancient herbs and spices, various smokes and other concoctions, brews and other fermented drinks, to the modern use of pills and powders, had always been pervasive in human society. What was new and different about modern society was the fact that suddenly, as in the last half-century, particularly in the great nation but, to a lesser degree in the rest of the world, those powers controlling society had decided to criminalize the use of certain drugs. Not all drugs, not the drugs of preference utilized by the ruling classes, but rather those drugs primarily in use by the lower and poorer classes of the society. With this criminalization came severe, mandatory prison sentences, along with increased police numbers, arrests and prosecutors, insuring higher numbers of convictions for these "crimes".The result was the guaranteed criminalizing of large numbers of otherwise non-criminal poor, predominantly minority youth. These young people, usually African-American and male, poor and uneducated, sweep into a cycle of arrest and imprisonment, were filling the many new prisons at an alarming rate. In fact, the prisons were filled with young Black and Hispanic inmates. It seemed as though the new social program that the great nation had adopted to confront the issues of poverty and education among the disaffected and the poor, was incarceration. As a result, the great nation, once renown for its humane treatment of its citizens, now had more people in prisons than any other nation on earth. The land of the free had become a land of tenuous freedom.

The runner had now been in continuous motion for approximately an hour and a half. The body continued to function in a smooth, coordinated fashion; his wind was good, his breathing free and easy. His legs felt okay; no unusual aches or pains outside of those to be expected in a long run. His mind was fresh, not weary. After all, he was only approaching mile thirteen. During his months of training, as his conditioning had improved, he had considered twelve miles to be a fairly easy distance. It was a distance that he considered to be at the lower end of the long runs; a little longer than ten, but not even at the half-marathon distance. Therefore, he was not intimidated by the distance. He was not expected any trouble achieving the distance and, in fact, none was forthcoming. With a burst of energy and confidence, the runner approached, then passed the twelve-mile marker.

chapter twelve: foods

"Into mile thirteen ...", thought the runner. And with that thought, he broke into an expansive, ear-to-ear mental grin. There was even the wisp of an upward curl upon his lips. In keeping with his usual habit, the runner was once again thinking in terms of being in the thirteenth mile, eschewing the twelve miles completed. The thirteenth mile, of course, meant that the halfway point of the long run was soon approaching; not an insignificant event. For from that point forward, the mileage covered would be greater than the mileage remaining; the countdown, albeit initially fleeting and cautious, was on. But this was, once again, getting ahead of one's self. We were, the runner cautioned himself, only at the beginning of mile thirteen, at least seven or eight minutes away from thirteen-point-one. Stay focused. Don't get ahead of yourself. Unbridled anticipation was the constant enemy. There was nothing worse, more frustrating than to be mentally a mile or two ahead of one's self. The danger of slipping into that mode of thinking was that, at some point, one realized that he had yet to actually run those mentally completed miles. And that realization resulted in the unpleasant phenomena of reality having to catch up with illusion. The body had to complete the miles that the mind had already deposited into the runner's account. This was, in effect, running those miles twice, the height of frustration. This was why it was so important not to get ahead mentally; to stay focused on one's actual position in the race. Try though he may, the runner had never discovered how to mentally make miles disappear without actually running them step-by-step. As a result, he forced his mind to abandon thoughts of the half-marathon point and to center, instead, on the beginning of the thirteenth mile. Focus on the passing scenery; the trees, the road, the buildings, the sky. And just keep running. Seventeen, eighteen, nineteen, twenty ... thirty, fifty, a hundred; counting steps again — start over again. One, two, three ...only a thousand to go to the next mile marker.

The runner knew through the experience and monotony of countless long training runs that, for him, there were approximately six-hundred to eight-hundred paces in a half-mile. In one of those extremely familiar runs that he had made a thousand times, one of those runs in which he knew every tree, lamp-pole, crack in the road and broken tree-limb. Where he knew the exact mileage from countless calibrations with his automobile's odometer; to pass the time one day and help the run to be over, he had counted the steps in a half-mile. Six to eight-hundred; he could not remember the precise number, or maybe he had lost count, or had achieved slightly different results on different courses. Six to eight-hundred paces equaled about a half a mile. This was useful information. Often, when the runner was travelling and running in strange, new places, he initially had no idea how far he was running. He could estimate by using his running watch, the Timex Ironman

Triathlon, but that estimate was based on an uncertain running pace. He knew that, depending upon conditions and his current fitness, the pace could vary quite a bit. In those instances, counting paces would provide a reasonable alternative. In long races such as the marathon, counting paces was a sometimes interesting diversion which resulted in covering small chunks of mileage. The problem for the runner was that the counting, itself, would eventually become boring and redundant; his inventive and calculating mind would sometimes become uncooperative and, of its own volition, start calculating larger, unpleasant figures, such as the number of paces to the finish. That number was usually so large as to be discouraging. Another trap to be avoided. The mind games were sometimes so complicated!

As the runners rounded a bend in the road, the course of the marathon had meandered inland, to the interior part of the city. The course had taken the runners into a large city park. Many cities in the great nation invariably were imbedded with great urban parks; large masses of land set aside for the transcendental and psychological good health of the denizens of the city. These parks were usually quite lovely and included such nuances, aside from the many trees and meadows, such as lakes, duck ponds, museums, golf courses and jogging and nature trails. The park in which the runners now found themselves was all of these things. For the runners, however, one characteristic stood out: hills.

Although the mid-western city was relatively flat, in geological and topological terms, with no identifiable hills or mountains in the region, for runners, a rise of ten feet represented a hill, albeit small. Road running invariably made the participants extremely sensitive to even the slightest changes in elevation. What might seem to be perfectly flat to the lay person, could be rolling hills to the road-runner. People, the runner had found, in their normal capacity, were exceptionally inattentive to changes in the landscape. People, the runner had found, were, as a general rule, inattentive, period. While motoring in one's car, most persons, even runners, failed to notice slight upward and downward changes in elevation. Running that same road, however, was a different story. Then one noticed even the slightest change. The longer one had been running, the sharper the focus, particularly on elevations. Driveways were hills, as were traffic bridges over and under railroad tracks and other streets. Every city, no matter how apparently flat, had long stretches of gradual inclines and declines. And runners noticed every one.

In marathons, where these hills occurred was of paramount importance. If they occurred during the first ten miles, no big deal. If they occurred in the last five miles — agony ! Anywhere in between and the emotional and physical impact of the hills depended on other factors: the steepness of the elevation; the length of the hill or hills; the number of hills; the relationship of uphill grades to downhill grades and the fitness of the runner. In certain marathons, very steep hills, of even a short duration, were known to the runner as "spirit-breakers". When one encountered such hills, often it was an intense struggle simply to reach the top; and when one did, leg muscles would be burning and the head would be symbolically screaming. One's pace would slow dramatically, almost to a walk, and recovery from the ascent would be slow and arduous. The hills of many marathons were famous for their challenging nature. Perhaps, most famous was Heartbreak Hill of the Boston Marathon, actually a series of hills beginning just after the seventeen mile mark and continuing through the twenty-first . These hills received their name not because they were, standing alone, particularly steep or difficult, but rather because of where they occurred in the race: mile seventeen. At a point when serious fatigue was setting in; when the "wall" was about to appear for many runners. If one was on the edge, close to that intangible barrier of fatigue, four miles of rolling hills would certainly take you over that edge, smack into the wall. They would "break your heart" !

Of course, all of these reactions were dependent on the fitness of the particular runner. Those in great shape, the world-class marathoners, hardly noticed the hills. The veteran amateur marathoners who had run many of the long races and who always did their training homework, also handled the hills well. For the great bulk of the runners, however; those somewhere in between the neophyte and the Olympian, whose training regimen varied from race to race, the hills could be either a break in the monotony — or murder.

In the current race, into the thirteenth mile, in the great and glorious city park, with its trees and gentle brooks, the hills broke mostly monotony rather than spirits. They were neither long nor steep, and after several short rolling peaks, ended almost as quickly as they had appeared. The runner had always enjoyed the phenomena of hill running. Not because he liked running hills, as some runners did, but rather because for some reason unknown to him, he seemed to do it well. He always seemed to pick up speed on the uphill grades and, in the process, pass many runners. He did not understand why or from where this ability had sprung, but he did not question providence. He just ran the hills.

In the process of running the hills, the runner found himself, for the time being, running alone. He had left behind many of those with whom he had been running and had not yet caught the next pack of runners. Solitary running was the essence of the existential running experience. It just the runner, the road and nature. Just your thoughts, the run and life; the moment that captured the essence of life and defined the meaning of existence. The meaning was the run — and the run was the meaning. Albert Camu, eat your heart out. Jean-Paul Sartre never had it so good. There it was, clear as a bell — life in a run, on the run, for the run. Amen, Brother!

In a race as large as the present one, one was never alone for long. If one increased the pace, one would quickly catch the next group of runners. If a steady pace was maintained, one would either run with a pack of similarly paced runners or other, slightly quicker runners would overtake you. In these long, heavily populated races, pack running was a rather unique experience. Often, through the long duration of the race, one would run with several different groups. In the various groups, for all manner of different reasons, one would notice distinguishing characteristics of the different runners. Perhaps, a colorful shirt, a distinctive running style, an unusual appearance, tall or short runners, attractive females, muscular men, long hair, baldness, ugly clothes, weird costumes and wonderfully fit, hard, athletic bodies. Runners were, as a rule, some of the best looking people on the planet. Nary an ounce of ugly body fat. Trim, sleek physiques, healthy, clear skin and wonderfully bright eyes. It was, indeed, a joy to be included in such a group. During the course of the race, the pattern was for one to see many of the same runners over and over again. Often, early in the race, certain of these runners would fly by, swift of pace. Later, depending on their level of fitness, one would pass the same, once swift runners, now paying the price for too swift a start. Sometimes, one would have extended periods of running with the same group of runners; perhaps four or five miles or more with the same fifteen or twenty runners. During this group running, different runners would periodically take the lead while others would follow closely behind. This was sometimes called "drafting"; it allows the following runners to be pulled along by the lead runner. It gives the following runners the sensation of easier running. On a windy day, it has the added advantage of blocking the wind for the fortunate followers. Fairness would dictate that the runners would take turns at leading the pack. In the large marathon, however, these spontaneous relationships were not so clearly defined and leading or following was often a haphazard affair. Interestingly, in these extemporaneous packs, relationships would sometimes develop between and among the runners. Brief conversations, of few words in duration would sometimes occur, resulting in a exchange of names and information. If the relationship endured longer than a few miles, the runners involved would often seek each other out at the finish line and exchange numbers and other information. Undoubtedly, many a romantic affair got its start in the middle of some long, grinding race. Love will find a way.

Now out of the hills, the runner mentally relaxed and let the race flow. He imagined that he was well over half way to mile thirteen. All was well. The body was responding favorably to the demands of the long run. The runner was very conscienous in his treatment of his body. Over the years of training and vigorous exercise, with the voluminous reading of the many journals, articles and books on physiology and running, the runner had come to be very cautious in the foods that he ingested. He had taken to heart the old but accurate cliche that "you are what you eat". More importantly, he had come to realize the immensely important impact that foods had on one's good health and vitality. In his studies and observations of the eating habits and general nutrition in the great nation, the runner had come to be astonished by the way the majority of citizens ate. For beginners, most of the citizenry was overweight. In fact, the prevailing attitude in the country was that being a little overweight was healthy. Or, perhaps, more accurately, a large number of those folks who were somewhat overweight either did not believe themselves to be such or rationalized away their condition. To be fifteen or twenty pounds heavier than one's ideal weight was, to most, acceptable. Denial was the norm. The runner, however, knew better. During an earlier time, in another life, figuratively speaking, the runner had, himself, been about thirty pounds overweight. He had learned, firsthand, the agony of carrying around a couple of bowling balls everywhere one travelled. Being married to the fat. He had known the misery of looking into the mirror with terror and disgust, of seeing a strange, bulbous, fat person on the other side of the window; a person with rolls of fat around the waste and a growing double chin between mouth and shoulders. Worse, he had felt the little aches and pains that accompanied the sedentary lifestyle. Particularly, his lower back had generated a chronic nagging, dull pain.

Although not totally to blame, he now attributed many of his former physical problems to his frequent consumption of jumbos cheeseburgers, fries, shakes, chips, ribs, fried everything and whatever else was on anyone's menu. Of course, at the time he had considered his eating habits to be quite good. After all, he was eating three squares a day, lots of beef, plenty of dairy products and good, wholesome milk. Eggs and bacon for breakfast, ham and cheese sandwiches for lunch and, if fortunate, steak and potatoes for dinner, with all the trimmings. Ummm — delicious! And deadly. Not that he hadn't been exposed to a better way. Early in his adult life, the runner had been exposed to many concepts of good diet and nutrition. He had conversed with many vegetarians and had taken to heart much of what their espoused. Indeed, he had, for a short time in his youth, embraced the lifestyle. He had not, however, persevered. As a young athlete, first in high school and later in college, he had sat at the training table many times and absorbed the latest thinking of the day regarding nutrition and performance. Much of what he had learned at that time, however, was flawed. In those days, the general "good health" doctrine included drinking three glasses of milk a day; it also included two eggs and sausage or bacon for breakfast and three full meals a day. Most doctors of the era did not know or did not consider the connection between these high fat foods and heart disease, cancer and other maladies. Not that certain others had not made the connections; there had always been those who preached moderation in eating, along with regular exercise. Most folks of that era, however, believed that eating discipline of that sort was only for young athletes in their early twenties. And the athletes, themselves, to a large degree, believed that they were immune from any deleterious effect from over indulgence. To a large degree, the runner had been among this group. Only the overweight and disgust of his early thirties, along with its companion, low self-esteem, had motivated the runner to seek a better way; to reexamine his life to find the answers to contentment and happiness. Once he had begun the search, the answers were so abundant, so readily available, so ubiquitous as to defy imagination.

What had begun as a simple attempt to lose some weight became, for the runner, an exercise in enlightenment. As he began to read the books and pamphlets, almost magically, the answer to good health through diet and nutrition, as well as exercise, unfolded before him. Lower cholesterol and fat intake, eat leafy green vegetables, do not overcook foods, lower salt and refined white sugar intake, avoid dairy products and eggs, red meats and pork and drink lots of water. It was simple, easy — and it worked. 1,500 calories per day and watch the weight evaporate. Ten, fifteen, twenty and finally, thirty-five pounds in three months: fantastic. The runner had found that there were so many foods and dishes that he liked that he only had to choose the healthy ones to engage in "nutritional discipline". That and count calories. He became so good at identifying the number of calories in different dishes that soon he no longer needed his tables and charts. Healthy eating became an integral part of his lifestyle. That and running. And slowly but surely, that bolbous, fat man in the mirror became the trim, sleek, firm, sexy, healthy and happy man soon to be approaching the half-marathon mark.

The bucolic beauty of the large , natural expanse in the midst of the city, gave the runner a sense of peace and good being. The leaves of the beautiful, ancient hardwoods russled in the gentle breeze. The large old trees provided shade and protection to the runners from the now bright morning sun. The road was smooth and flat. Ahead, as a local rock band belted out a lively, Bob Seger tune, amidst the usual gathering of race-type folks, was the thirteen mile marker. The runner, however, strode forcefully past this marker, intend on yet another, more meaningful sign just down the road. For just ahead, highlighted with a large, digital display clock and a single white line across the road, was the thirteen-point-one mile sign. A slight tingle ran through the runner's body as he thought with satisfaction — half-way home!

chapter thirteen: marriage

High times and exhilaration! Let the good times roll! As Ray Charles would say, "I wanna roll with my baby...". That and so much more excitement and satisfaction characterized how the runner felt at this moment. There was something special about thirteen-point-one, the half-marathon, reaching the halfway point. Symbolically and psychologically, for the runner, reaching this milestone in the race was huge. From this point forward, he would have covered more territory than that which remained. He could now think in terms of distances less than a half-marathon, a distance that he always considered imminently doable. Additionally, the runner felt a sense of achievement in having completed a half-marathon. Although he knew that always the last half was more difficult than the first, much more difficult, in fact, having completed the first half gave him a good feeling. The half-marathon was, itself, a considerable distance. In road-racing circles, it was a distance held in high esteem. All of the great world-class runners ran half-marathons. The runner could cite the world records at that distance for both men and women. The times of those superb athletes, however, were so fast as to be, for the runner, at best unbelievable and at worst, a depressing reminder of his snail-like pace. At such moments, he had to remind himself of the millions, no — billions of people in the world who could not run even two or three miles at any pace; then he felt better.

For the moment, however, he felt great! Having run multiple marathons before, the runner had fully expected to be generally feeling good at this stage of the race. He had trained many times before for marathons. He knew as the race day approached how his training had gone. He knew whether or not he had trained sufficiently to run the distance. He knew, based on past performances, generally what to expect of his body. He had run marathons when his training had been insufficient; he had paid the price by dying in the race. He had also run a number of satisfying marathons, running strong throughout and finishing strongly. If he trained correctly, he expected to go the distance. In training, running twelve, fifteen or even eighteen miles, as one built up strength and stamina, became easier to do. One did these distances many times in the typical marathon training period. As a result of this training, one lost the fear and anxiety about running these distances. The result of the rigorous training was that one had confidence and efficacy about running these distances. One believed that he could do these distances easily. There was a catch, however. Indeed, there were several "catches" — flies in the ointment, as it were. The pace at which one trained was invariably slower than the pace at which one raced. The difference could be as much as two minutes per mile in pace, which translated into the difference, for example, between a two-hour-forty-minute marathon at a six minute-per-mile pace and a three-hour and thirty-minute marathon at an eight minute-per-mile pace. Depending on one's ability and conditioning, the pace at which one ran could vary tremendously. Also, at shorter distances, a runner might be accustomed to running at a much faster pace than was advisable in a marathon. Always, in the marathon, the internal conflict that the runner had was balancing the pace against the distance. How fast could one go in the marathon and still finish running? World-class runners could run the marathon distance at almost the same pace at which they ran much shorter distances. Often, these runners would average under five minutes-per-mile for an entire marathon, indeed, an incredible feat. Of course, in addition to their innate athletic ability, these runners usually ran more than a hundred miles per week in training. Training and running was all that they did. For persons such as the runner, who earned their living doing other things, who had "ordinary" jobs, to be able to train at fifty miles a week for six to eight weeks was a major accomplishment. For such persons, running a marathon might happen once a year, or less. To attempt to run these long races at the faster, "short race" pace, would be almost suicidal. Because, however, for such runners attempting to run marathons was generally so infrequent, because their experience was so limited, pace mistakes were common. In marathons, large and small, the sight of exhausted runners walking after eighteen miles or so was, indeed, common.

The other "catch" was atmospheric conditions on the day of the race: weather and altitude. A hot day could change everything. If the temperature was over sixty-five or seventy degrees, to finish the race, one had to run at a much slower than projected pace. Often, runners failed to make this adjustment ... and hit the wall. If the race was run at altitude, that is , higher than sea-level, or higher than one's training site, the oxygen would be thinner and, thus, times would be slower. Again the runner faced the danger of running out of energy prematurely. Wind was the other great factor. If it was strong, as in above fifteen or twenty miles-per-hour, and if it was a headwind, particularly during the latter stages of the race, it could be a significant factor. Driving rain, cold weather and even ice and snow could be factors as well, since marathons were never cancelled. All of these components had to be factored into each runner's calculation as to how fast he or she could run the long race. It was a delicate calculation, as a ten or fifteen seconds per mile adjustment could be the difference between running a great race and walking at the finish.

Fortunately, for avid runners, there were many marathons run in the great nation and around the world, in all different climates and at all different times of the year. Therefore, for the astute runner with a little flexibility, the choice of marathon could reduce greatly many of these variable and insure a much higher probability that conditions would be at least close to those in which he had trained. Such was the case for the runner in the current race. In fact, the runner was from an area not far from the great city, with similar weather and altitude. He had, over the years, learned to pick his marathons carefully. There had been times, painful memories, when the runner, in his enthusiasm to find a convenient marathon to run, had chosen races in climates other than that at which he had trained. Usually, this had been during the winter months. Because the runner had always lived in the more temperate regions of the nation, areas possessed of longer, colder winters, he had learned to run outside in cold weather. He had often run when the temperature was close to zero, on ice, albeit carefully and slowly, and in light snow. He had learned that when one dressed appropriately, with layers of the new, light, high-tech clothing, one could be quite comfortable in temperatures with wind chill factors as low as ten below zero Fahrenheit. The potential problem with this sort of training, with regard to running marathons, was that the body adjusted to running at that temperature and in those conditions. To attempt to run in dramatically different conditions, even though one had run successfully in the newer conditions previously, was an exercise in futility. In the normal course of events, seasons change gradually; in a training scenario, this allows the body to adjust to different climatic conditions without the trainee actually realizing those changes. Going instantaneously, however, from one climate to another, can have a profound and often disastrous effect on the athlete. The runner had learned this the hard way. On several occasions, he had attempted to run "warm weather marathons"; races run in the southern regions of the great nation that had an almost sub-tropical climate. That meant warmer weather and higher humidity. This had proven to be, for the runner, a grave mistake. With his body unadjusted to the warmer, more humid climate, although the runner invariably felt great at the beginning of these races, he invariably made the mistake of setting a pace far to quick for the conditions. The very predictable results had been the "death march" being played around the sixteenth or seventeenth mile. Remarkably, it had taken the runner three of these disasters over a six year period to figure out the problem. He had learned that one must either dramatically downgrade one's expectations in these situations, running so slowly as to turn these races into "training runs", or, as a better alternative, chose races that more closely simulated one's training conditions. In deciding on today's race in the great city, the runner had taken the latter road.

As the runner strode forward, midway through the fourteenth mile, feeling good and with no major problems or tell-tail signs of fading or slowing down, his mind, once again drifted. Over the years, the runner had noticed that while running, one often thought of other problems that one had in life. This was, of course, not unique. What was interesting, however, was the fact that often during this running contemplation of life's daily problems, solutions were forthcoming. Many times while running, the runner had come upon ideas about how to solve the problem of the moment. He would then attempt to repeat silently this remarkable solution until he finished his run, got home and could write down his idea. This phenomena had happened many times to the runner. He was not quite certain why this happened although he had his theories; perhaps, because running stimulated the flow of blood in the body and, in following, in the brain, thoughts were facilitated. Perhaps, the block of solitary time that one spent running aided the thought process. Maybe it was some combination of the two. He didn't know. What he did know was that the process existed and that he was the occasional beneficiary.

As the mental drifting process continued, the runner had thoughts of his wife. Although the runner had participated in many relationships during his years of life, he had been married for only the last few years. It had occurred to him at some point in mid-life, that in order to experience the greatest benefit from a relationship, one had to make the greatest commitment. He had decided that in order to experience the highest level of love and happiness, one had to do more than simply "date", "shack-up" or "go" with the other person. There had to be a higher, symbolic commitment to the other person. In this society, the most obvious manifestation of that higher level of commitment in interpersonal relationships was the institution of marriage. As a young man, the runner had shunned the idea of being married to another person. He had rejected as archaic and antiquated the idea that one must have the state sanction one's relationship of love through marriage. He had, at the time, thought those ideas to be backwards and non-progressive. However, with the passage of time, and with a broadening scope of experiences, his ideas on the subject had evolved; not changed, per se, but rather had risen to a higher level. He had realized that marriage, although at one time distasteful to him for various youthful notions of freedom and politics, was a time honored institution at whose base was the deep commitment and love of a man and a woman. He did not eschew same-sex relationships or the rights and dignity of the people involved but, for him, the relationship of preference had always been heterosexual. And in that context, both historically and currently, marriage represented the ultimate level of love and bonding with one's partner. The idea that one swore an oath to the other party to love and honor gave marriage a higher level of meaning on the relationship continuum; the fact that being married was state-sanctioned, while not adding any intrinsic value to the relationship, nonetheless, gave that bond a higher meaning and value because of the heavy societal pressure involved in the relationship. The fact that by marrying another, one exposed one's self to a certain amount of discomfort and unpleasantness at the prospect of ending the relationship, inherently made the relationship far more serious than a passing infatuation. That, in itself, made one realize that this was a circumstance not to be taken lightly. One had better be certain of what one was doing in taking the marriage vows, otherwise big trouble and complications lay ahead.

The meaning and deepness of marriage, however, transcended the realization of possible legal complications associated with ending the relationship. The glory and wonder of the relationship was indelibly interwoven in the bond and love that developed between the participants. A bond at whose roots were the duty undertaken by the parties to one another; the duty to love, to understand, to listen, to compromise, to be silent when one urgently wanted to speak, to agree when silently one disagreed, to smile rather than to frown, to speak kindly and softly, to hug as needed, to caress when called upon and, of course, to love frequently and willingly. Marriage required of its participants constant vigor and creativity in order to maintain an interesting and exciting relationship. Too often the runner had witnessed friends and acquaintances allow their marriages to slip away into the hopeless abyss of monotony and boredom due to their lack of understanding of the input necessary to sustain the relationship. It was an unfortunate reality that in the society, many of the mores and behaviors that were associated with marriage were based on conceptions of unexciting routine and negativity. Television shows and movies had often depicted marriage as a necessary evil for the production of family, with the parties having a distant, mundane relationship devoid of love and, more importantly, sexual excitement. The idea had been put forth that sexual excitement and heart-pulsing lust were properly left to young singles and honeymooners, not "old married people"; they, the older marrieds, were supposed to be content with a more platonic, cerebral relationship; a relationship grounded upon a pleasant, largely untouching toleration of one another, with time being occupied with job, same-sex diversions, gardening ,golf and grandchildren. Societal expectations of the marital relationship were, in fact, very low and somewhat unappealing. These expectations, while not universal, were widely accepted; they were also, the runner knew, largely in opposition to how love through marriage should function. These expectations were to be disparaged. Marriage should be fun! It should be at the apex of relationships. Everything that made relationships exciting in one's youth — baited-breath anticipation, sexual excitement, happiness and love — should be magnified in marriage. Marriage was and is a tremendous opportunity to experience all of these wonderful things both on a daily basis and for a lifetime. It simply requires the same type of commitment that one is taught to input into other areas of life. It requires that one apply the same rules of good behavior, respect and courtesy that one would utilize with strangers, with one's spouse. Marriage requires the same attention to detail that the project at school or work commands. It is the ultimate expression of that old and wise cliche: "you reap what you sow". The more one injects into marriage, the more one loves, the more one cares, the more one sublimates one's own concerns in favor of the other, the stronger and more beneficial the relationship. In short, the more love that you give, the more love you receive. Strong love begets strong love, and life becomes exponentially sweeter and sweeter.

While the runner's steps were still relatively light, although his body did not cry out in agony, while he continued to feel well, he was concerned. Experience told him that, approaching the fourteen-mile marker, he was getting deep into the race. He was approaching the danger zone. A time in the race when, physiologically, anything could happen. Yet, he continued to run easy and feel good. Ahead, fast approaching, were the familiar tables, volunteers, drinks, vasoline and the like. Accepting two cups of water, one for drinking and one poured over the head, the runner perambulated past the fourteen-mile mark.

chapter fourteen: drugs

Passing the fourteen-mile sign, the runner could not help himself, despite his self-imposed rules, of briefly thinking:"... only twelve miles to go...".These thoughts, of course, were in flagrant violation of his laws against thinking too far ahead in the race. He was thinking in a manner deleterious to his running and psychological good health. The penalty for such indiscretions could be very serious and far-reaching; they could be painful and emotionally harmful. Nonetheless, the runner briefly thought of the mileage yet to be traversed. It was a distance that seemed not quite so imposing. No longer was he looking at twenty-six miles; it was now twelve, which was barely more than ten, which was just a run in the park — a moderate training run. The end was not quite so far, not quite so long, not quite so distant. He was making real progress!

And yet, as quickly as these thoughts occurred, that familiar mental policeman in the runner's head reappeared and quickly banished all such thoughts. Think only of the next mile, nothing more. Forget about race's end; it did not exist. Only the next short goal and nothing more. Stay focused! A brief positive thought about the finish was okay, so long as it was brief and positive. The danger of which the runner was well aware was that the thoughts of the miles to go could far too easily turn into negative thoughts; thoughts of how far the finish line was, and how long it took to run twelve miles. Too easily the thoughts could be converted into images of difficult twelve-mile runs, of which the runner, and every runner, had experienced many times. Too easily those thoughts could become admonitions and rationalizations encouraging the runner to discontinue the race; banish these thoughts, stay positive and keep running. Feel good and be the road.

Into the fifteenth mile, although the race was beyond the half-way point, the majority of the runners were showing few signs of weariness. The fool-hearty entrants, those who had no business entering the long run to begin with, had long since dropped out of the run. Their numbers were generally small, as the length of the race served to have a chilling effect on frivolous entries. For the majority of the runners, the idea was to finish the race running. Therefore, these athletes were prepared to go the distance; they had trained to go the distance and were, barring unforeseen catastrophe, well able to do fifteen miles with relative ease. There was, however, a slowly growing rate of attrition. The race, the relentless miles, were beginning to slowly but surely take their toll. The weak were gradually falliing by the way-side. There were the runners who had attempted to do the race despite being injured. Always, these runners existed; in fact, the runner had, himself, attempted races, even marathons, while being injured. The scenario was always the same. During the course of the heavy training and long runs that were routine in marathon preparation, often, for a myriad of different reasons, runners would incur injuries. Almost always, these injuries were the result of overtraining; attempting too much too soon. Sometimes, the injuries were caused by ill-fitting or worn out running shoes. Having the right shoes in marathon training was a delicate proposition. Although the technology in developing durable, well-cushioned running shoes had advanced in the runner's lifetime to an almost unbelievable degree, nonetheless, when running forty, fifty or sixty miles a week, shoes worn out quickly. Not worn in the ordinary, layman's sense of the term; shoes with a lot of sole left, that looked good and were perfectly appropriate for washing the car or a picnic, were often no good for long runs. Indeed, shoes that were fine for short runs of five miles or less were, likewise, dangerous to use for long runs. In the pounding that the feet had to withstand in a run of twelve miles or longer, the slightest irregularity in a shoe could result in wide variety of injuries; bad knees, shin-splints, blisters, Achilles problems and several different hip problems were merely the tip of the injury iceberg. The particular runner had the misfortune of never knowing with certainty that his or her shoes were gone until he got a signal from his body. The hope was always that the signal would be benign rather than debilitating; that any injury, when it occurred, would be of a minor nature, requiring only a few days of rest to heal sufficiently to allow a resumption of training without a loss of conditioning. Experienced runners, acutely sensitive to the signals that their bodies sent out, and also immediately responsive with healing strategies at the first sign of injury, were usually able to prevent serious injury and continue a successful training program. However, for those runners who ignored these early signs, who failed for whatever reason to replace worn-out shoes promptly, who attempted to "run through" certain injuries that required rest, the injuries became more serious. For many of these runners, however, the thought of not running the marathon for which they had trained so assiduously, was more than they could bear. So, when race day came along, they ran in spite of their injuries — and paid the price. They had rested for a few days before the race and were feeling better; better, that is, when they were walking around. In the race, however, around the tenth, twelfth or fifteenth mile, their injury would recur and, eventually, they would break down. At that point, they knew that running the marathon in their condition had been a mistake, but their pride and motivation took over and they pushed on, limping and walking, walking and limping, occasionally running a few steps, desperately attempting to somehow finish the race. Visions of a great time had long since been vanquished; the goal now was to simply cross the finish line.

Into the fifteenth mile, a few of these misguided runners were beginning to appear, limping along the side of the road. They numbers, however, were as yet small. The vast majority of runners were fit, healthy, injury-free and running strong. At mid-race and feeling good! The runner happily counted himself among that number. He had, in the last half-mile, gone through a period, as he was prone to in the long runs, of self-monitoring; checking familiar body functions, running mechanics for early, tell-tail signs of deterioration. Unusual weariness in the upper thighs, slowing down perceptibly with the inability to increase speed, a general, overwhelming fatigue ... all possible early signs of hitting the wall; none were present. The runner was grateful for his physical strength; the rhythmic gait of his stride was smooth and even. He was cautiously beginning to think that maybe, just maybe, this was going to be one of those memorable, good marathons; one in which he felt good from start to finish, ran strong all the way and, consequently, experienced high self-esteem and warm feelings of accomplishment for weeks afterwards. Maybe this would be one of those races, one of those glorious days! Maybe...

The earlier cloudy skies had given way to a brilliant sunshine in the autumn morning. Perhaps, too brilliant and too sunny for many of the runners, desirous of a bit less solar heat. For the runner, however, the sun was nice. He liked to run on sunny days, provided that the temperature was not too high. On this day, those were the conditions, with the temperature in the low to mid-sixties. This was almost ideal for the runner. He felt good.

The course of the race had turned once again, now traversing a more commercial area of the great city. Specifically, the course was now taking the runners over a small bridge above some old, infrequently used railroad tracks, vestiges of another era, before airlines and interstates, when the railroad was king. The now abandoned tracks served as a reminder of how quickly passed notoriety and importance in a dynamic and rapidly changing society. Ironically, almost directly adjacent to the tracks was the new, gleaming interstate highway, better known as a "freeway" in the city. Out with the old and in with the new; that was the way of the modern world. Tear down the old and, perhaps, the

not so old, to be replace with the latest fad in building construction. Construction fueled the economy, produced jobs
and enriched contractors. Of course, new construction also
inevitably displaced poor, powerless people and destroyed
forever old, architectural masterpieces. Such, however, was
the way of the world.

Abutting the freeway were the ubiquitous signs. Signs
selling everything imaginable, from cars and computers,
cell-phones and salvation, to wines, liquors and beers. The
alcohol advertisements stimulated thoughts by the runner of societally sanctioned highs. Substances traditionally
utilized by humankind to escape the drudgery of the daily
grind. It was a curiosity to the runner how a particular society could, on the one hand, endorse, sanction and even promote certain recreational drugs while, on the other hand,
outlaw the use and sale of other similarly used substances.
The contradictions, to the runner, were glaring and obvious.
Alcohol, of course, was the most obvious drug of choice in
the society. Social drinking was a well established phenomena; the bars were everywhere, along with the liquors stores
and the neighborhood party stores. In many states in the
great nation, despite the disingenuous outcry by the often
inebriated politicians against drunk drivers, beer, wine and
even hard liquor was available at gas stations. Gas up the
car and juice up the body in one convenient stop.

In the society, a large proportion of the population drank
to some degree on an almost daily basis, with a significant
minority having some manner of an "alcohol problem".
Drinking was glorified in movies and on television; having
a beer or two with the boys during the football game or

after work was a well accepted ritual. For the more socially correct upper-classes, it was wine with dinner with an after dinner aperitif. For the brothers on the block, it was a forty-ounce beer or two or, perhaps, some cheap wine. Almost everybody drank something alcoholic at some time and in some place. Less publicized but no less pervasive, was the society's addiction to over-the-counter and prescription drugs. Every household had a ready supply of morphine-laced painkillers. Most also had a ready supply of uppers and downers, more correctly known as diet pills and tran-quilizers, also called amphetamines and valiums; all legal and all in great supply. The use of patent medicines in the society was of monumental proportions. These were the unregulated drugs available at the neighborhood phar-macy or supermarket. The aspirins, acetaminophens, ibu-profens, inhalers, antacids, laxatives and other strong and yet readily available drugs in common use in the society.

The use of drugs in society did not represent an unu-sual behavior in society, or something unique to modern culture. To the contrary, drug use in human societies was as old as the existence of human culture. The use of strong potions derived from natural sources, such as roots and herbs, dated back to the earliest of human societies. Fer-mented beverages, likewise, had a long and storied history. Wines and beer-like drinks, such as mead, were a well doc-umented part of human history. Modern society had only refined and up-dated humanity's passion with high-induc-ing substances. There was, however, one uniquely modern twist to this old equation: modern society had taken upon itself the task of criminalizing on a wide scale the use of certain high-inducing substances and drugs. This modern phenomena had resulted in the wide scale criminalizing and imprisonment of large numbers of the young, male underclass population, usually members of societal racial and ethnic minorities and poor, who derived from sub-cultures in the great nation whose recreational drugs of preference, although in wide scale use, had been deemed illegal by the white, European majority that controlled the political power structure of the nation. While the society rationalized it harsh and draconian drug laws by citing the harm that these drugs reaped upon their abusers, in reality any abused substances, legal or otherwise, reaped similar harm upon those who were the abusers. Society also rationalized these harmful policies by pointing to the condition of the neighborhoods in which these drugs were popular; neighborhoods plagued by crime and poverty. Of course, society chose to ignore those learned scholars who repeated pointed out that the excessive drug use was the result of the poverty rather than the cause. Not lost on the runner was the fact that almost all of those suffering the impact and effect of these harsh drug laws were racial and ethnic minorities, laws exclusively promulgated by the racial majorities of the economic upper classes. It had occurred to the runner that these drug policies might, in fact, be a manifestation of policies specifically designed to oppress potentially troublesome minorities and poor peoples; poli-cies made easier and, perhaps, validated by the centuries-old social and cultural racism that existed in the great nation. These policies by the great nation, elicited memo-ries of the runner, of earlier cultures that had been plagued by the evils of the economic, social and racial oppression of large segments of its population. Often this oppression had been implemented by the promulgation of laws with severe penalties that had a disproportionately harsh impact on the oppressed segment of the society. Often these laws were cloaked in neutral language and justified by pretext ally enunciated morals and ideals. Often the masses of the majority population in these societies had either chosen to accept these pretexts as factual or had buried their collective heads in the sand, ignoring the obviously oppressive impact of these laws. Only time and history had exposed the folly of their ways and the devastating impact of those "laws". Only time and history had exposed the oppression and corruption and held these societies accountable for their harsh and unjust treatment of their own citizens. Only time and history had condemned majority populations for their passive complacency in the midst of this oppression. Perhaps, the runner thought, some future society would look back upon the great nation with historical curiosity, and wonder why the majority population had allowed such obvious mistreatment and oppression to exist. Perhaps not.

The road had suddenly changed to concrete, much harder on the feet and the body. The pounding of the surface had brought the runner's thoughts back to the task at hand. Usually, race planners and directors designed the race courses to avoid these hard surfaces, but sometimes, for whatever reason, they occasionally appeared. This was such a time. Particularly sensitive runners could not long endure such surfaces and injury would result. Fortunately, in this case, the course took a sharp turn and the surface of the road was, once again, asphalt. With that turn came into view the usual collection of people and tables, music and bands playing, with water and gatorade being dispensed. The sign simply read: "15".

chapter fifteen: illness

Fifteen miles. A noteworthy distance. From one end of Manhattan Island to the other was shorter. The runner thought about his days as a New Yorker, thinking what a pity that he was not a runner at that time. Oh, he had occasionally pretended to be a runner, or rather, a jogger. He had, from time to time, attempted to run around the reservoir in Central Park, a distance of a mile and a half. Usually, in those days, with the smoke of many a Kool cigarette in his lungs, and various nefarious substances in his body, he was able to go only a few hundred yards before, gasping for air, he would have to stop and walk for a while. He would then start up again, and so forth until he finished the run, the monumental mile and a half. Actually, he walked most of the distance. But, he supposed, at least he had attempted the feat a few times. In some elementary way, those gasping, short runs were the forbearers of his current marathoning. For even though he had been woefully out of shape, even though he had never succeeded in actually running around that reservoir in those days, he had laid the mental groundwork for his future as a long distance runner. He had at that time, unbeknownst to his youthful self, planted the idea in his long-term memory that running was a good and worthy thing to do; that setting goals of certain distances and, at least, attempting to complete those goals, was a desirable thing to do. He remembered that even in those days when he had rarely finished a run, by his current standards, when the distances that he was attempting were extremely modest, despite his youthful age and demeanor, he had, nonetheless, achieved a sense of satisfaction in the effort. He remembered that his friends of the time had been impressed with even the modest effort that he was making. Running was, even in its infancy in his young life, a positive thing.

And yet, as he pondered those early days in New York, he could not help but feel a certain sense of remorse and disappointment about the many terrific runs that he had never done. He had always felt that New York City was an exciting and marvelous place. From Ellis Island and the Verrazano Bridge, linking Brooklyn and Staten Island, to Harlem and the Bronx, with its wonderful Zoo and broad avenues, New York City was a singularly unique city. Even the name had a certain flair to it: New York City, "the Big Apple"; "New York, New York ... so nice they named it twice!" With its concrete canyons and hot, funky closets, also known as apartments, with its perpetual traffic jam below Fifty-ninth Street and millions of hustling citizens, with its ethnic, cultural and architectural diversity, its 164 museums and 10,000 restaurants, New York was, indeed, an exciting, sexy, vibrant city. Of even greater importance to the runner was the tolerance toward different kinds of people for which New York was famous. Amidst the veneer of the sneering cabbie and the cold, pitiless concrete, lay a city noted for its acceptance of people of all descriptions, races, religions and life-style preferences. New York had room, figuratively speaking, for everybody. Say what you would, dress as you chose, it did not matter in the great city; the rules were the same for everybody: pay the rent or leave. No pity in the Naked City. Meet that threshold, however, and everyone was welcome; a novel idea in these modern times.

The runner had returned to New York in his later years, after he had cleaned up his life and had began running in earnest. He had relished running, not walking around the reservoir, marveling over how short the distance actually was. The difference in perspective was amazing. In these later years, he had often looped Central Park, running along the outer road that circled the park, a distance of approximately six and one-half miles. This was something that he had never dreamed of in his earlier days. Now, he could run the distance with relative ease. Life was, indeed, a wonderfully strange phenomena. He had also run in the New York City Marathon. The New York Marathon was a marvelous, unique race, with upwards of twenty-five thousand participants. The runners were from every state and probably half the countries in the world. It was a wonderfully cosmopolitan affair. It traversed all five boroughs of the City, bisecting in the process, some of the more interesting neighborhoods of the City, including Williamsburg in Brooklyn, an Orthodox Hassidic Jewish neighborhood where the men wore long, black coats with long, curly hair and long beards, First Avenue on the east side of Manhattan, the urban "chic" capital of the world, and down Fifth Avenue in Harlem, the unofficial capital of Black America. In the race, one encountered runners speaking many different languages, with t-shirts and jerseys representing running clubs from across the globe. There were so many runners in the race that one was virtually always in a crowd, an unusual condition for a twenty-six mile race, but probably appropriate, considering the city and its reputation. Because of those conditions, it was not a race where one expected a fast time; nonetheless, it was a truly unique running forum, one that had to be experienced to be appreciated.

Despite having done the New York Marathon once, and despite having run a few miles around Manhattan on his recent visits to New York, the runner, nonetheless, regretted the city runs that he had missed. Considering himself to be an urban road runner, he relished the idea of running, for example, the length of Manhattan, doing the shoreline of Far Rockaway in Brooklyn along Reis Beach, Flatbush Avenue, Prospect Park and Eastern Parkway and, of course, the many bridges of New York. He contemplated how he would have enjoyed exploring on foot the many hidden and otherwise unknown neighborhoods of Manhattan or running down the Grand Concourse or Cogan's Bluff in the Bronx. Perhaps, he thought, there would yet be an opportunity to do these runs. Currently, the task at hand took center stage.

Passing the fifteen-mile mark or, as it were, barrier, was another one of those intangible milestones in marathon running. Fifteen miles was a distance that the runner often used as a training run in preparation for the marathon. It was a distance that, in his mind, truly represented the threshold of the really long-distance runs. It was a distance that one had to absolutely be in excellent condition to achieve. It, figuratively speaking, separated the "men from the boys...", in the broader, non-sexist sense of the term. One could not simply get up in the morning, roll out of bed and run fifteen miles. The distance required much effort and diligence. It was not, nor would it be taken lightly.

It was, therefore, with an ensuing sense of purpose and a guarded sense of accomplishment that the runner strode into mile sixteen. Fifteen miles; it had a symmetrical ring to it. You knew that you had done some running when you hit fifteen. It was a time in the long race when self-assessment was, once again, revisited. Fifteen was far enough into the race that if physical deterioration was going to happen, signs might now be present. Seriously tiring legs and an accompanying slowing of the pace were the dreaded signs of an impending "wall". Conversely, it was equally signifi-cant to be feeling really good at this juncture in the race. If one hit the fifteen mile mark running strong, with a light and bouncy step, with legs and body not complaining too much, with the mind cooperative and positive, even enjoy-ing the scenery and the entire phenomena of running of the marathon, that was a very good sign. That was an omen of, perhaps, good things to come. Perhaps. Caution was, once again, required. The runner knew all too well that the "wall" could yet be cleverly hidden around the next bend in the road or, perhaps, a couple of miles hence. The finish was yet eleven miles away, a considerable distance. Nonethe-less, completing fifteen and feeling good was a very posi-tive sign.

The weather remained ideal. The wind was light and not a factor in the running; the temperature was moderate, in the low sixties and the sun was peeking out occasionally, without being oppressively arrogant Indeed, a nice day for a run in the park. The runner, reassured with his good physical presence in the race, once again allowed his thoughts to drift. Recently, a good friend, a companion of many years, had been diagnosed with a life-threatening illness. This friend was now engaged in a struggle against this affliction to survive and recapture his life and vitality. As the runner had grown older, slowly and subtly, he had begun to take note of the number of his friends and associates who had become ill. Not illness as in a cold or the flu but rather gravely ill, as in cancer, heart disease, diabetes and other life-threatening afflictions. Almost always, the persons becoming ill purportedly had no warning, in a physical sense, of the ensuing illness; one day they were healthy, the next day sick. Or so it seemed. The runner had noticed, particularly among his closer friends who had become ill, those persons with whom he had a closer knowledge of their lifestyle, that upon closer examination, almost always there had been tell-tail signs of impending poor health. The obvious lifestyle signs had been smoking and excessive drinking of alcohol; where these were present, eventual illness was almost inevitable. These, coupled with the lack of a daily exercise regimen, were the obvious factors in illness. The runner had found, however, that in addition to those well-known risk factors, there were latent, more subtle factors that were usually present in those persons who had become ill. These were factors which, when only moderately present, were generally not considered health risks. Factors such as very moderate drinking, ingesting large amounts of sugar in coffees or processed foods, being moderately overweight, particularly relative to the individual's ideal weight and, of course, eating high fat, high cholesterol foods; foods often considered to be wholesome and healthy and not necessarily "junk foods". On the other hand, the runner had observed many persons of moderate habits and healthy living patterns, who were vital, healthy and happy as they aged, avoiding the major illnesses. Often, in the races in which he had participated, they were older runners. People in their sixties, seventies and eighties, running races of all lengths, including marathons. These inspiring persons served as the runners role-models; he wanted to emulate their lifestyles and approach to older living. The problem, as he saw it, was that too few persons actually continued to live active lives as they aged. He knew that most of his friends did little or no exercising whatsoever. They sat at a desk all day, considering a round of golf as exercise, even though they rode in golf carts. The runner worried about his friends; he wanted them all to live long and happy lives. Perhaps, somewhat selfishly because he, too, wanted to live a long time; he wanted the company of his cherished friends. He had quickly decided, however, that if wishing good things for other persons was a manifestation of selfishness, at least in this instance, such selfishness was permissible. Let us all get old and happy together!

One continual observation regarding illness that the runner had was the reality of a strong, inverse relationship between a positive attitude toward life and the occurrence of illness. People who were constantly happy and positive about life, about the day-to-day happenings that constituted living, seemed to have fewer problems with illnesses of all kinds. They were less likely to suffer from colds and the flu and, it appeared that they were also less prone to the major illnesses. The runner had also observed that to a person, all of the really old folks that he had known had a tremendous lust for life and wanted to live. No negativity on the part of these remarkable persons; they were bound and determined to continue living — and they did. Length and quality of life, he had found, were indelibly connected to the desire to have a long and happy life. It was a case of mind over matter, with a happy ending.

With good thoughts of his good health and better fortune, the runner focused, once again, on the road ahead. Things, he thought, were going well. His head was clear, free of those potentially agonizing thoughts of the miles to go, instead centered on the positives of the smoothly functioning, finely tuned machine that was his body. He took a few deep breaths, which resulted in a momentary surge of energy, an old trick of the experienced runner. The air felt good in his wide-open lungs. He felt no exhaustion or wanting for wind; only good thoughts and good feelings. Passing the tables and people, the runner chose to forego the water and drinks as he entered the seventeenth mile.

chapter sixteen: wealth

Sixteen down — ten to go; at this point, the race was at a very serious juncture. Into mile seventeen, this was serious marathoning. All thoughts of a leisurely run in the park on a lovely day had fallen by the wayside. The race had reached a point where any hint of frivolity had dissipated. From this point forward, the race and the running were all business. The adrenalin rush that had accompanied the earlier miles of the race was now gone. No longer could the runner float along solely on psychic energy, being pulled along by the flow of the race. Other considerations had taken precedent. It was now time for some blue collar, grind it out, down and dirty, gut-level running. No cute running tricks or strategies would predominate now; sixteen miles had ended all illusions of cuteness —fundamentals now were key: conditioning and pacing. Eyes forward, smooth strides, remain focused.

The runner was keenly aware of the potential dangers of these next few miles. In the past, when he had encountered trouble in marathons, when he had "hit the wall", it had come between miles sixteen and twenty and usually in the seventeenth mile. This was a critical mile. The runner knew that although he was currently feeling good and running well, the crash could happen, as it sometimes did, virtually without warning. He could well remember flying through the first sixteen miles at the Boston Marathon one year, feeling terrific and running strong, only to rapidly deteriorate and crash at the base of the "Heartbreak Hill" at mile seventeen. Heartbreak Hill in the Boston Marathon had obtained legendary status in running circles as one of the ultimate tests in marathoning. The "Hill" was actually a series of gently rolling hills that occurred on the marathon course between the seventeenth and twenty-first mile. These hills, standing alone, were not particularly impressive or difficult from a running perspective. They were not steep and there were plenty of gentle downhill segments to counterbalance the uphill sections of the hills. What made these relatively gentle inclines "Heartbreak Hill" was their location in the race, coming seventeen miles deep into the race. This is the point in a marathon when a runner can began to experience serious tiring. Well-conditioned athletes, as an essential part of their long distance training, learn how to "run through" difficult phases in a marathon, where the mind overcomes weariness of the body and the runner continues to run. Often in marathons, this phenomena occurs around the seventeenth, eighteenth or nineteenth mile. Get through this "zone" and one usually experiences a revitalization after the twenty-mile mark. Entering this zone is a time in the race when the somewhat weary runner can least afford to deal with extra stress and challenges. It is at this critical juncture in the Boston Marathon that one encounters four miles of rolling hills — Heartbreak Hill. Many a fine runner has met his demise in these four miles; the transition on the faces and in the paces of the runners in Boston is a remarkable study in agony and determination simultaneously. It has been said that "the Wall" was invented at Heartbreak Hill. The runner, like the many, had experienced the wall at Heartbreak. The onset of the wall had been so rapid that the runner literally did not realize what was happening until it was too late and he was walking. Not that there was anything that he could have done to prevent the crash once it started. By then it was too late and the real agony of marathoning began. The walking and jogging; attempting to reduce the agonizingly long, long miles to the finish line. Run for five minutes, walk for ten. Run to the next street light, the next block, the big tree in the near distance, then walk again. This sequence would repeat itself until, finally, the finish line banner would appear overhead in the distance. Then the thoroughly fatigued runner could usually muster up enough reserve mental toughness to run the last few yards and finish the race with a modicum of dignity. This was the truly tough part of marathoning. Running a great race, running all the way and finishing strong, was fun; it was almost easy. One felt good throughout the race and even better after the finish. The true test of character in a marathon came when, as in life, things did not go as expected. Finishing a marathon after hitting the wall was much more difficult and testing than running the flawless race. As with difficult times in life, the lessons one learned from this trying experience, the finishing of the race under the most adverse of conditions, served one well in his or her future endeavors, be they running or simply negotiating life. Those who survived that experience and returned to the fore to try again were invariably better, stronger and wiser runners. Those who survived were, likewise, better, stronger and wiser persons. They were better for the experience and, in following, the world was better for their heightened contribution to the whole.

As the runner traversed a curve in the road, he realized that although in the past mile seventeen had occasionally meant disaster, in the present race he was running smoothly. No extraordinary pain or fatigue exhibited itself — he continued to feel good. All signs were cautiously positive. Reassured by his good fortune, the runner, once again, allowed his mind the luxury of drifting into other thoughts. He thought about the nature of running and how, in the one sense, the phenomena of running was so wonderfully egalitarian. All one had to have to run was some sort of running shoes. In fact, the shoes were even optional. The runner thought of Abebi Bakila, the great Ethiopian marathoner of the nineteen-sixties, who had won two Olympic marathons in succession, the first of which he did running bare-foot. One did not need fancy, expensive equipment to run. Nor did one need to belong to some exclusive club or gym to get involved. All one needed was the desire to run, to get into shape. Simply open the front door and partake; the world was your fitness club. Unlike so many other systems and structures in modern society, it mattered not what one's wealth or status was with regard to running. All were welcome. The benefits were consistent for all.

In life, unfortunately, the structures and systems were not so just. In all societies, to varying degrees, there were the haves and the have nots; the rich and the poor; the sunny side of the street and life "across the tracks". Currently, the great nation was in the midst of a long, sustained economic boom. Many of its citizens were experiencing the economic times of their collective lives. The rich had become the fabulously rich, the middle-class had become, at least in terms of lifestyle, the rich and the lower classes had, to a lesser but, nonetheless, significant degree, become middle-class in their lifestyle. The great nation seemed to be riding on an endless seventh wave of wealth and prosperity. Wealth and the pursuit of money, had taken on a new meaning and significance in the collective psyche of the nation. Once modest people were now feverishly trading stocks on their home computers; popular movies trumpeted the credo of "greed is good"; houses were getting larger and more lavish, and cars were, as in the 1950's, once again becoming larger and less fuel efficient, as in gas-guzzling SUV's. Mutual funds had replaced savings accounts as the primary repository of disposable income as the nation had collectively thrown caution to the wind. It was a true economic frenzy, dressed in designer clothes and riding in an air-conditioned, wood-trimmed, leather-seated Lincoln Navigator.

In the midst of these good times, it seemed to the runner that society had, somehow, lost touch with basis philosophies of wealth and societies. For the past two-hundred years or so, contemporary society had been dominated by variations of two classical economic philosophies: capitalism and socialism. One, which the great nation followed, was based on the individual accumulation of wealth, while the other, once popular in other regions of the world, was based on the equitable distribution of wealth among all people. The one philosophy had at its foundation the idea that the accumulation of wealth by individuals was a good and desirable thing; that the motivations and behaviors necessary to become wealthy also had a positive impact on society; that "market forces" would serve to weed out undesirable conditions in society, would drive out of business inefficient and corrupt entities and businesses and, as a result, what would be left would be the cream of the crop. By association, this cream would, because they were the cream, would also exhibit the highest of behaviors in other non-economic areas such as morality and humanistic concerns and, thusly, make society a better place for all. This philosophy carried with it the idea that the less governmental regulation the better; that the economic marketplace would be self-regulating. The other economic philosophy carried with it a basic skepticism that human nature, left unregulated, would not exhibit the proper concern and compassion for their fellow human being. That "the market", left unchecked, would enrich a few particularly ruthless and driven individuals to the detriment and impoverishment of the remainder of society. Its central theme was that it was better for the greater good of society to control the flow of commodities and wealth so that all individuals, regardless of their business acumen, were guaranteed the basic necessities of life; that all persons in society would have jobs, a nice place to live, food, health care and a standard of living consistent with the overall wealth of society. These philosophies, as manifested in one ideology or another, had been in basic competition world-wide, for the past one-hundred and fifty years. The more recent labels for these ideas were Capitalism, usually with a democratic political system, and

Communism, usually with some sort of autocratic political system. Of course, the underlying ideas encompassing both philosophies had been around for all of recorded history. The basic ideas were sharing versus hoarding; helping one's fellow man as the primary philosophy versus helping one's self first. There had been many variation on this theme throughout history and millions, perhaps, billions of words written and spoken over time supporting the one or the other. The result was a confusing boggle of ideas and ideologies, customized to suit the momentary top dog. The runner was confused by all of the cross claims and accusations made by the various ideological zealots. He only knew that he believed in sharing and happiness for all humankind. He only knew that he believed that no person should want for food, shelter or clothing, or any of the basic necessities of life. He had seen that life sometimes had an unfair and unjust impact on an individual's ability to be monetarily successful, though they be faultless. He had seen entire groups of people left out of the economic success mix, though they be faultless. He thought that any good and fair system ought to account for these conditions and provide a strategy for the correction of these conditions. And he thought that for any economic philosophy to be viable in the final analysis, it ought to have in its forecast a feasible plan for dealing with all of humanity world-wide, rather than just a few favored nations. Beyond that, the philosophic mumbo-jumbo of the oft heard economic gurus only confused the runner. The road ahead was a far more desirable alternative.

chapter seventeen: philosohy

As the runner passed the seventeen-mile marker, still feeling good, he, once again, had a momentary burst of optimism. He knew that he was getting closer to that magical twenty mile mark; he knew that he continued to feel strong; he knew that these were all good signs. He could remember with relative ease those races when his condition had been otherwise. In fact, he could readily remember walking past seventeen. He could recall the brilliant, blue sky and the hot sun beaming down upon his head in Jacksonville, Florida, one Sunday morning. The humidity and temperature had sapped the energy out of his body, reducing his gait to a slow walk. The southern sun had once again denied him the good race that he had expected; the good race that he had trained for in the northern reaches of the great nation. On three or four different occasions, the runner had made the mistake of training for a marathon in one region and running the race in a different, warmer region. The reasoning was understandable; one did not want to run a marathon amidst a northern winter, with wind chills below zero. In fact, for the most part, they did not exist. Marathons held during the winter months were, invariably, in the warmer regions of the country. From early December until late March, almost all of the long races held in the great nation were either in the southern or the western areas of the nation, where the weather was milder during the winter months.

The problems that the runner had encountered with warm weather marathons were primarily those associated with the acclimation of the body to climatic changes. Northern winters in the great nation, although becoming milder in recent years due to one reason or another – perhaps, the "greenhouse effect" or, perhaps, due to a natural warming cycle – were, nonetheless, cold enough to have a serious impact on training and running. With actual temperatures routinely in the teens and twenties, and occasionally dropping into the sub-zero range, winter running, and in particular, the rigorous training required for the marathon, was difficult at best and often impossible at worst. The runner, as with most serious marathoners, preferred running outside to the monotony of training on a treadmill in some fitness center. There were many problems associated with training exclusively on a treadmill, not the least of which was finding a treadmill available for hours of use at one time. Most fitness centers often had time limits on the time each person could use the treadmill. Then, there were the logistical problems incumbent with going to a fitness center; travel time, showering, crowded conditions and the like which were not a factor when running at home, outside. Finally, the actual task of running on the treadmill was, in and of itself, very different from running outside. First and foremost, one had to be careful not to fall off or misstep on the narrow belt of the treadmill. The runner often enjoyed gazing about while running, taking in the scenery or simply drifting absent-mindedly. Such behavior was a big "no-no" on a treadmill. There, one had to concentrate on striding straightly and staying on the belt. Drift slightly left or right and one faced a potentially serious fall off of the machine. In addition, the runner had found that each treadmill was calibrated at a slightly different speed, making precise pacing somewhat more difficult. He had found that his comfort zone on a treadmill was more difficult to achieve, that maintaining a faster pace, comparable to those that he ran outdoors, was harder to do. And, of course, there was the tremendous monotony. To the runner, twenty-five minutes on the treadmill was like running an hour outside. The constant drone of the motor, staring at the same wall or window or mirror or whatever one was facing; every stride the same; speed constant; minor, manipulated changes in elevation; predictable programs; everything about the treadmill was monotony personified.

Not surprisingly, given this intense distaste for the treadmill, the runner did the majority of his training outside – even in the dead of winter. The result of this practice was running with multiple layers of clothing, long distances in bone-numbing wind chills. While doing this allowed the runner to get into marathon condition, it was a conditioning attune to severely cold climates. When, after this training, the runner attempted to jump on a plane, get a good night's sleep and run a marathon in sixty or even seventy degree temperatures, the results were, particularly in hindsight, disastrous. Hello Wall!! Crash!! Fourteen, fifteen or sixteen and out. What was amazing to the runner was the fact that the inevitability of these so predictable results had eluded him for so many years, over multiple efforts to run these warm weather races. Was he stupid... or just overly optimistic? Probably a little of each, plus a healthy dose of that runner's feeling of invincibility; that attitude that says that one can run anywhere, any distance, at any time. Me and Jesus can walk on water, climb any mountain and run any marathon, hot or cold, day or night... Bullshit.

Into the eighteenth mile of a marathon, the concentration of the runners has become more narrowly focused. This phase in the race is increasingly a time when the runners mental activities are centered less on superfluous thoughts, where there is less gazing at passing sights, where the idol chatter that was so prevalent in the earlier stages of the race, has all but disappeared. All eyes are centered on the road ahead. One can feel the intensity of purpose among the runners; it is so thick that it almost creates an aura unique to the latter stages of the marathon. For at this point in the long run, indeed, the runners have crossed an invisible, intangible barrier into the final reaches of the race. Eight miles to go. Walkers, those who have inadequately trained or who had foolishly started too quickly, are now starting to increase in frequency. They serve as a reminder to those still running of what might occur in their not too distant future. They serve also as a motivation to avoid a similar fate.

In this atmosphere, the runner continued on his epic journey through the city streets. It seemed to him at this juncture in the race, that the course had traversed every neighborhood in the great city; of course, his more rational self knew this not to be true, but rationale be damned, that was how he felt. Despite his growing fatigue, he was running at a steady clip, passing the walkers, along with those runners who were slowing down. He was able to gage the strength of his pace by the increaing frequency of those that he passed. He knew that he was still running good; he knew that so far, things continued to go well. His guarded optimism intact — his mind, once again drifted.

As his body was slowly immersed in a dull ache of fatigue, a condition familiar to all long distance runners and endurance athletes generally, his thoughts settled into the familiar territory of the oft asked question: why run marathons? More specifically and introspectively, why am I running twenty-six miles? Why do I find myself in the middle of the eighteenth mile of a marathon, running on some heretofore unknown city street at 9 am on an otherwise beautiful Sunday morning. For what purpose do I run? Surely, one could find a more enjoyable method to pass the time; surely life itself was not predicated and valued solely on one's ability to run marathons? Why, then run? Of course, to be in great shape, healthy and vigorous; of course, for the psychological satisfaction of having accomplished this formidable feat. But was there a deeper, philosophic underpinning to the marathon? Was there a connection to the introspection that accompanied the long run and the meaning of life, itself? These thoughts led the runner to yet deeper thoughts of philosophies and ideas associated with that eternal quest for the meaning of life. The runner's life had been largely defined by an endless search for philosophic justification and meaning of life. That journey, over the years, had carried to runner to many places in the travelogue of the mind, stopping briefly or enduringly at many unique or mundane locations. Existentialism, as introduced through the works of Jean-Paul Sartre and Dostoevsky, had, at an earlier time, dominated the runner's innermost thoughts. Did life have meaning? And, if so, what meaning? After several years of agony, the runner had rejected that philosophy as being, in its final analysis, too negative and suicidal. It had proven to be contradictory to the runner's lust and joy of life and living. The runner, as he discovered, was an incurable romantic, not well suited to depression and thoughts of suicide that went hand in hand with existentialism. Philosophy, however, remained an integral part of the runner's life. Not the philosophy taught in the logic classes at the universities, with their highly structured arguments, assumptions and presumptions. Rather, the philosophy that at its essence, highlighted thinking about ideas and beliefs as they related to life and its living. The philosophy that accentuated identifying the wisdom of living rather than the mathematics of logic. The philosophy that centered on learning about life, on separating good ideas from bad, wisdom from folly, and the pursuit of wisdom from reckless egocentricism. The philosophy that clarified life and, by doing so, glorified living.

Most people in society, the runner had found, had no personal, self-generated philosophy of life. Of course, if you posed this question to people, they would, no doubt, have an answer and a philosophy of life to reiterate to you. They would, no doubt, quote the "Golden Rule" or some other religious expression; or, perhaps, some other cliché or witticism about life that they had been exposed to for life – something that their father's father had told them; or maybe something that they had heard in church, or on talk radio, society's latest universal pulpit. The runner had long since realized, however, that these expressions of supposed philosophies of life for most people, were merely or rather simply ideas adopted by masses of peoples from the current popular propaganda (i.e., religion) without thought. People had adopted the explanations for living as well – all without any process of internal analysis. Indeed, the so-called philosophy of life exhibited by most people, sophisticated as well as simple, powerful as well as impoverished, was simply a manifestation of "blind faith"; ideas adopted without thought or justification, adopted as the result of societal pressures, peer pressure and generational socialization. In the final analysis, most folks had no internally developed, well thought out philosophy of life. Most people simply lived their lives according to the pattern developed and structured by others. They simply accepted the popular beliefs and dictums about life as gospel, without for a moment questioning the validity of those beliefs and ideas. In fact, most of these self-same people would vigorously defend those same, unexamined ideas, sometimes to the death. Often in wars, people were sent off to die for ideas that they hardly knew and certainly did not understand. Curious. The runner thought of these things with a profound sadness. He had long since rejected the "blind faith" syndrome. He believed that it was important for people to think about life and its true meaning. It did not matter if people agreed on these things; it was important that they thought about these ideas before accepting them as gospel. Closer inspection of basic ideas and philosophies, the runner strongly felt, could only improve society. Thinking about the ideas that formulated the bedrock of societal philosophy enhanced one's personal sense of responsibility to society; it enhanced one's sense of accountability for those ideas, good and bad and, eventually, elevated good ideas and rejected the no so good. It made life better — this was good.

These thoughts brought a smile to the runner. They were good thoughts; they had helped to make the long run just a little shorter, just a little easier. Ahead, with fewer people and less fanfare was the eighteen-mile marker. Secure in his thoughts, mindful of his philosophic harmony, the runner grabbed a cup of water and ventured onward.

chapter eighteen: feminism

Gliding past the eighteen-mile mark, the runner regaled happily with the reality that he continued to feel good and run smoothly. He realized that even in a marathon as close to perfect as one dared hope for, there would be moments, perhaps, a quarter, a third or a half-mile at a time, when the running would be extremely hard and one's resolve would be tested. He had not yet hit that plateau, but he knew that, inevitably, it would come. And yet, at the moment, things were fairly good. Into the nineteenth mile — seven to go. More importantly for the runner's personal goals, less than two to go to the magical twentieth mile. For him, the marathon was all about running through the twentieth mile. Get to twenty running and he had it made. In all of his many marathons, he had always finished strongly, running all the way to the finish line when he had made it through the twenty-mile barrier running. There was some intangible essence, a combination of strength of character and motivation, that kicked in after twenty. That, along with the notion that the end was getting much nearer, seemed to drive the runner after twenty. He did not clearly understand the phenomena; he only knew that it existed. It seemed almost to have a life of its own, akin to "the force" in Star-wars. Whatever it was, the runner's faith and confidence in the phenomena had grown with successive positive experiences; the reinforcement had been so great that the concept had become, to a large degree, reality. Get to twenty and you've got it made!

Of course, the runner quickly reminded himself, you've only just passed eighteen. Still almost two miles to go before twenty — two long and serious miles. Miles that could become step-by-step ordeals, if the runner was not careful. He feared that possibility; it was the worst case scenario and made for the most difficult running; when one became acutely aware of every step in a mile, or half-mile, or even a block or two. Then the distances became much longer; one became more conscious of time and, as a result, the entire process seemingly became much slower — agonizingly slower.

Remarkably, the weather had remained excellent. After the brief showers earlier, conditions had stabilized to a partly sunny, beautiful day. The wind, always the potential enemy of the runner, had remained relatively benign, gently blowing at under ten miles per hour; strong enough to be pleasantly cooling and yet not hindering or deleterious. The sun was very much in evidence, a condition that, no doubt, displeased some of the competitors. However, with the billowy clouds occasionally providing a reprieve, not a relentless or overly oppressive condition. As the runner strode his way into mile nineteen, he noted with satisfaction that the weather could not be better. Mother nature had done her part and answered those unspoken prayers of all of the runners to provide good weather; it was now up to him to do his part.

The course was now making its way through one of the many ethnic neighborhoods in the great city. There were signs about in what the runner surmised to be Italian, touting various food products. Small, seemingly intimate little restaurants lined the compact blocks, tightly packed with small commercial enterprises, interspersed with apartment flats and lofts. This, the runner thought, was truly a largely self-contained, urban ethnic neighborhood; the sort that were rapidly disappearing in the great nation. They were becoming an anachronism, a vestige of another era, rapidly dissipating with the changing residential patterns of the great nation. Instead of the close contact of these old ethnic boroughs, modern neighborhoods tended to be developed communities, often with gates and guards and overly large, identical and impersonal houses. Communities with infrequent contact among neighbors, if any. This was the modern trend, the ideal of the young, upwardly mobile couple in the great nation. It seemed sad to the runner that the nation, in the name of modern progress and increased individual wealth, was losing much of the ethnic intimacy and diversity upon which much of its heritage was based. Progress marches on, leaving culture and history in its wake. It was the modern trade-off, like it or not. The runner quickly decided that he liked it not.

Into the nineteenth mile of a marathon, even runners in superb condition began to feel the strain of the long run. This strain affects different athletes in different ways. Some, perhaps most, simply slow down. Others resort to a wide and often bizarre range of behaviors to deal with the onset of this great fatigue. But always with the runner, the ultimate goal was to break the distances down to smaller and smaller segments. It seemed easier to the runner to cope with those hard times in the long race by looking ahead, figuratively speaking, only a hundred yards at a time. Complete that hundred and then do the next hundred yards. On and on until the crisis passed and the running once again became easier. As strange as that might sound, it kept the runner focused on the immediate and restricted his mind from pondering negative thoughts concerning the great distance to the finish line. Bizarre as it may seem to the uninitiated, it worked; it got the runner through the hard segments of the long, long run.

As the runner approached what he calculated to be about the halfway point in the nineteenth mile, he focused his attention momentarily on the group of runners around him. As was often the case in these long runs, there were certain runners who seemed to be running at about the same pace as the runner. It was a curiosity to the runner how this phenomena played out. Sometimes in these large races, one would see a certain number of runners throughout the race. Perhaps, early in the race the runner would notice several runners grouping and running with him for a mile or so. He would notice their dress or particular physical characteristics and, though unspoken, they would become his friends and running soul mates. Eventually, as with most relationships, the bond would be broken when one of the protagonists would increase his or her pace and disappear into the abyss of the large group of runners. Oddly, however, often the same runners would magically reappear much further down the road. It was almost like a marital reconciliation, a class reunion, a renaissance. Once again, the road would be shared with an old companion. And there was joy in the recognition. Hello, old friend! I am happy that you continue to share this adventure with me! Let us pool our collective psychic energy and stride these next few miles together. Often, it provided the necessary surge of energy to complete the next mile; it was a welcomed diversion.

But, in additional to the usual observations, there was something particularly compelling about this group of runners. One of the joys of running was the company that one kept. One's fellow runners were almost always interesting people. They were usually successful, well-balanced folks, with a very positive attitude about life. Of course, they were extremely healthy and, usually, the epitome of athletic attractiveness. Particularly the women. Invariably, the female runners had great bodies; low body fat, sculpted figures that would do justice to any pictorial in **Playboy**. The runner had joined a group that included several such female runners, running smoothly with halter tops and bare midriffs. They were looking good! For as long as he could remember, the runner had always admired beautiful, attractive women. He thought that, among other things, one of the great joys in life for a man was the sight of a beautiful woman. Perhaps, for woman as well, one way or another. But the runner, being a progressive thinker and having a liberal mind, was also acutely aware of the fact that in certain feminine circles, the sort of admiration of the female physique of which he was currently partaking, was considered a manifestation of some sort of sexist, male-chauvinist behavior. From this prospective, these seemingly innocuous observations became an assault on womanhood. And the observer became, by association, a mental criminal, as assault had always been classified as a crime.

These thoughts, and certain aspects of feminist ideology, had, at times, caused the runner great perplexity. He had always believed in equal rights for all people; in particular, equal rights for those persons in society who, historically, had been denied them, i.e., minorities and women. He had actively supported the feminist movement from its earliest contemporary nuances; specifically, the women's liberation movement born of the 1960's. For him, this movement was a natural offshoot from the Civil Rights Movement for African-Americans and, as such, one worthy of the highest level of support. However, there were several aspects of that ideology with which he had difficulty. There appeared to him to be an apparent dichotomy, a contradiction of sorts between the feminism philosophy stressing the equality in all aspects and on all levels between the sexes and the development of happy and healthy heterosexual relationships. One of the great joys of life was the advent of a loving relationship between a man and a woman. Beyond initial infatuation, however, for these relationships to endure on a long-term basis, the individuals involved had to accept their roles in the relationship. Often, the roles were and are based on sexually specific behaviors. In other words, the man had to do man-type things while the woman had to do woman-type things — both doing so willingly and joyfully. When these roles are understood and accepted, happy relationships exist. When they are resisted or denied, relationships, despite the best of intentions, wither away and eventually end. Of course, the runner understood that these concepts were not terminally juxtaposed. He understood that modern relationships could encompass aspects of both ideas successfully. But he also understood that often the concept of equality was misinterpreted. The root of the term from a moral, philosophic and political perspective, dealt with equal treatment under the law, equal access to the wealth and riches of society and equal respect, dignity and status. Equality never meant that either all people had equal ability or that people were not meant to have dominant or recessive roles in society, families or relationships. It was okay for one person to allow another to take the lead in certain areas. In a relationship, this was not necessarily a manifestation of inequality, but rather role-playing — the understanding and enactment of which was critical to the successful, long-term relationship. It appeared to the runner that the lack of understanding of this delicate balance between moral equality and pragmatic role adjustment was at the root of the many divorces and unhappy relationships that now plagued the great nation. That and a pronounced lack of good **sex.**

It appeared to the runner that a clash existed between what he perceived to be male and female chauvinism, with a resulting tension that made long-term relationships difficult. In fact, female chauvinism, with its apparent male-bashing character, seemed to sabotage healthy heterosexual relationships. There seemed to exist a certain correlation between hardcore lesbianism, the feminist movement, male-bashing and the diminution of healthy, long-term heterosexual relationships. To the runner, the existence of these relationships, while undeniable, was likewise complex and confusing. That they existed was clear; how they interacted was not. These thoughts had succeeded in carrying the runner down the road. Ahead was the 19 mile marker.

chapter nineteen: sports and athletics

Striding smoothly, the runner glided by the 19 mile marker. The marker was a big, white three foot by five foot piece of plywood with large, black numbers. Immediately beside the marker was a digital clock giving the running time of the race. Both of these items were fairly common in the galaxy of road racing. Some races did not include the digital clocks, leaving the participants to their own devices to determine their times and paces. Other races sometimes did not have markers at every mile. This was a more serious oversight, which could cause the runners great anxiety. In these long races, the psychology of the runners was very delicate. The expectation was that there would be a marker at every mile. The runners came to depend on these signs. In fact, they were extremely important to the participants to reassure them that their pace was correct. When these signs were missing, the runners would panic. One could hear the exchanges: "…have we reached the 19 mile mark yet?", or "This is a really long mile". Worry could easily creep into the minds of the runners that something was wrong with their performance. In a marathon, worry could easily become a self-fulfilling prophecy: one more thing to worry about in the long race. No one needed this! Fortunately for all the runners on this day, in this race, this was not an issue, as both markers and timers were included at every mile.

The significance of the passing of nineteen miles was not unnoticed. Of course, at this point in the long race, nothing relating to the physical running of the race went unnoticed. For the first time in the race, the runner could contemplate the finish line. Seven miles to go was not a scary prospect to the runner. Seven miles, after running nineteen, was no joke... there were certainly plenty of things that could go wrong. However, in the normal course of training for the marathon, the seven mile run was not considered a long run. Indeed, the runner usually thought of seven as a rather benign distance. It was below the double-digit threshold and just beyond the friendly five mile distance. It was normally an easy distance; one that the runner could consider without great trepidation. The end was getting closer!

The weather continued to cooperate. The skies were predominantly clear and the temperature remained a tolerable 70 degrees. The wind was a light but refreshing ten miles per hour; as a bonus, currently a tail wind. At this point in the race, it appeared almost a certainty that the weather would not be an overwhelming factor in the race. Now, it was only about finishing the race— and finishing strong!

The azure sky floated languidly above, as if etched upon the pallet of life by the ultimate impressionist painter. Monet resurrected had joined the celebration of life that characterized the moment; itself having acquired an almost divine quality of countenance. Twas, indeed, a beautiful day! Thoughts such as those currently filled the runner's head. It was moments like these that separated running from all other forms of exercise and made it unique. At these times, philosophic thoughts dominated one's essence and one experienced a catharis. It was no longer about the physical act of running; no longer about simply being fit; no longer about cardio-vascular good health, weight control, lower cholesterol and the like. In these moments, running was akin to a religious experience. It was an epiphany. It was the essence of being. It was being one with God. Running, at these all too brief interludes, almost transcended life itself. What a rush! Inevitably, however, the grind of the long run would overcome the beauty of these moments which, though seemingly eternal, actually lasted only seconds at best. The unevenness of the road, a gust of wind, a quick breath would break the wonderful spell of the moment and, regrettably, the runner is returned to the reality of the long run. Gone was the godhead, surrendering to the sweat and pounding of the road.

As the runner continued in his quest for the finish line, once again his attentions focused upon the runners around him. Around him, amidst the throngs of runners, his attention was drawn to several of the endless variety of t-shirts worn by his companions of the moment. He noticed that many of the shirts carried on them the various insignias of runners clubs. The shirts brought to mind thoughts in the runner of his experiences with athletic organizations from his early days as an impetuous youth. Organized sports, he realized, had played an important role in his life. In fact, the more he thought about it, the greater and more significant was the impact of the organized athletic experience on the quality of life in general and throughout time in memoriam.

His contacts had begun at an incredibly early age, due in a great part to the wisdom and insight of his parents. Almost from his earliest remembrances he had been exposed to some form of organized sport. Initially, it had been swimming lessons at the local YMCA at age three. As a youth in the great city there had once been many of these facilities available. Sadly, in recent decades, as the middle-class population base had moved out of the city to the suburbs, these institutions had followed, leaving in their wake a vacuum. Lost to the youth of the city was the opportunity to partake in the instruction and camaraderie provided by these organizations from which the runner had so greatly benefited. The benefit gained from learning at an early age the lessons of group activity, as well as the practical advantage of learning how to swim and exercise were, to the runner, immeasurable. The society was plagued with a permanent class of citizens who were sedentary and mildly obese. In fact, this class represented a majority of the adult and youthful citizens of the great country. A great part of these phenomena was attributable to the fact that great numbers of people had never learned how to exercise. They had not participated, due to unavailability or a lack of insistence by their early schools or their parents, in any kind of organized sport. As a result, they had failed to learn how to exercise; they had failed to learn what their bodies could endure physically. They had failed to learn that minor aches and pains were all part of the process of getting into shape. They had never experienced that wonderful feeling of euphoria that accompanied the afterglow of a good workout. They did not know how much further they could push their bodies beyond perceived thresholds of pain, or that the exceeding of such perceived barriers was a normal occurrence in athletic behavior and a critical component of human physicality. As a result, these millions of people became "couch potatoes", fat and out of shape. A heart attack or stroke waiting to happen, accompanied by an inability to live life to its fullest, constant complaints, limited physical abilities and eventually, sexual impotency. What a price to pay for a lack of early guidance and direction!

The benefit of early athletic training, the runner realized, was even greater than the physical well-being he had noted. The sport, and in particular the team experience, benefited people and society in another highly significant manner. The process of participating in a team setting taught the individuals involved that the benefit to the group was **more important** than individual achievements. Even in less than ideal settings, with uninsightful coaches or egocentric individual "superstar" members of the team, the other participates nonetheless benefited from the residual team experience. The members of the team learned that by channeling their efforts for the good of the team, the team would function more successfully and, as a result, bring notoriety and satisfaction to its members. The participates learned that to sublimate one's individual goals for the good of the team ultimately brought greater individual satisfaction. Additionally, in most instances, the participants learned life-long lessons of character and perseverance from their coaches. They learned that they could endure far more perceived pain and suffering than they had previously thought possible, without suffering any lasting impediments. In fact, they learned that the satisfaction achieved was well worth any pain endured. Little clichés such as "no pain, no gain" were phrases that one carried throughout life. And early coaches were remembered and revered throughout life as surrogate fathers who had taught great and lasting lessons of the importance of character and perseverance in life. Repeatedly, many an older, highly successful individual spoke in hushed reverential tones about how this coach or that changed his or her life after an otherwise inconsequential practice during a high school football season. The important impact of sport was undeniable. Sadly, too many missed this important experience. The runner felt fortunate that he was not counted among that number.

The noise jarred the runner's consciousness back to the task at hand. Ahead, amidst loudspeakers and rock music and volunteers dispensing water and sports drinks of various descriptions, was the large placard with the distinctive two- zero written across its face. This was it at last: Mecca. The twenty mile mark!

chapter twenty: alcohol: addiction vs. habitual behavior

Reaching the twentieth mile in a marathon is an accomplishment both symbolically and in reality. It is symbolically significant in that it represents a threshold beyond which the ultimate goal seems much more obtainable. Once one passes into mile twenty and up, an intangible barrier has been pierced. In a sense, confidence in one's ability to complete the race grows exponentially. Figuratively speaking, from that point forward, it's all down hill! For the runner, it was a rush;. that momentary sense of euphoria associated with a burst of adrenalin in the body that comes at various times in life. A much coveted feeling lionized by poets and songwriters. A very real feeling of well being. In running, those types of feeling were very important. Running a long race was a delicate balance between physical conditioning and mental stamina. Most persons who entered marathons were, to one degree or another, physically capable of completing the race. For those who had problems, it was often the mental woes that defeated them. They had run their twenty-mile training runs, had logged the necessary mileage and were lean and tight, probably for many in the best shape of their lives. Physically, they were ready for the race. They had adequately prepared for the run physically. Often, it was those mental, psychological demons that destroyed their good intentions. Creeping doubts, exaggerated feelings of fatigue, perspectives that made the road seem so much longer; doubts, doubts and more doubts… these were the nemesis of all runners. The little thoughts slipping into one's mind designed to prevent the completion of the race; thoughts that said: "…why are you doing this? …you're in great shape, this race proves nothing…running twenty miles is a sufficient accomplishment…it's okay to stop for a little while…" Those were the thoughts that had to be replaced with positive ones, designed to encourage the runner to finish the race. Thoughts such as: "…only a 10-K to go…I am feeling exceptionally good today…I am on pace to run an excellent time…my body is ready, willing and able to complete this marathon and I am going to feel really good afterwards."

As the runner continued, he overheard two runners just ahead discussing how good a couple of cold beers were going to be after the run. The mention of beer got the runner to thinking about the proliferation of alcohol in society and how casually most people thought about drinking alcohol. It was interesting to the runner how acceptable alcohol was in society while, by contrast, the penalties for using other drugs were severe. Marijuana, for example, in the state where the race was being held, was a four-year felony. Heroin and cocaine, so called "first class controlled substances" were punishable by up to twenty years in prison for a first offense. On the other hand, persons convicted of second-degree murder, if they behaved themselves in prison, could usually be released after eight or nine years. Such laws made no sense to the runner. The runner had abstained from the use of alcohol for twenty-five years. He knew of the tremendous potential for the abuse of alcohol, having himself experienced the phenomenon. He did not object to the use of alcohol by those who choose to do so and, in fact, occasionally enjoyed a glass of wine. What he objected to was the widespread concept in society that differentiated between alcohol and other drugs. The idea that there was some fundamental difference between these drugs which were legal and regulated and those that were illegal. This, of course, included the widespread advertisement and use of prescription drugs, which were advertised on television pervasively; as cure-alls, such as "soma" from **Brave New World** by Aldious Huxley. Alcohol was, in fact, by far the most abused drug in society, responsible for more illnesses and deaths than all other drugs combined. What made one drug legal and available to the general public, with certain restrictions, while the possession, use and/or sale of the others were felonies, was a cultural rather than a moral, ethical, criminal or logical decision. It was a decision fueled by the religious ideas and cultural habits of the founders of the society, with little or no regard for the cultural habits of other ethnic groups, as well as a total disregard for massive scientific evidence to the contrary. It was, in fact, a real life manifestation of the idea that my drug of choice is okay while yours is not. In fact, your drug is evil beyond belief, is responsible for all of the ills of society and is the bane of humanity. Your drug of choice is, in fact, a creation of the devil incarnate and you, if you use that drug, are an agent of the devil. As I condemn you, I'll have another double vodka martini. Interesting thoughts of substance abuse, as defined by society, mercifully interrupted by the sight just ahead of the twenty-one mile marker. Societal reforms would have to wait for another time, another day; the race was the thing!

chapter twenty-one: psychology

Mile twenty-one! The runner could feel the exhilaration surging through his veins like a vaccine or vitamins. As a drug addict receiving after long delay, a badly needed fix, the excitement was palpable! Mile twenty-one: only five and change to go. At this point in the race, with only five miles to go, it was acceptable to contemplate the finish line. Through experience, the runner knew that he was close enough to the end, that he had already completed twenty-one miles and, as such, the likelihood of his completing the marathon without hitting a "wall" were high. At this point, sheer will could carry the runner to completion of the race. It was a good feeling!

The mid-morning day was a thing of beauty. The shining sun was no longer a threat to the completion of the run. The temperature had cooperated beautifully; it was in the mid-fifties with a mild breeze. In fact, it was a drop dead gorgeous day! The kind of day that made life worth living; the kind of day that elicited thoughts of spirituality, of a supreme being. Since the runner did not believe in a "supreme being", or at least not one as enunciated by the major religions, despite his overwhelming joy at being alive and the beauty of the day, his approach and explanation for such matters rested on a more scientific approach. In his case, the study of psychology had, to a large degree, taken the place of religious explanations for natural phenomenon.

As an undergraduate, he had stumbled upon psychology while simply attempting to fulfill the various curricula requirements. His love affair with the logic, beauty and simplicity of the psychological explanation of human behavior had been comprehensive; so much so that it had become one of his majors. The psychological explanation of human reactions to the mysteries of life had, for him, eliminated religious explanations that heavily relied on mythological reasoning. Psychology, for the runner, had foreclosed the necessity, one which he had already rejected, of relying on rationalizations which included all-powerful, invisible beings as the sole reason for various occurrences in nature. For the runner, psychology had slain the bogeyman. The psychological concept of self-actualization had replaced religious concepts of heaven and life after death. It was, in fact, when achieved, a kind of "heaven on earth"; a condition much more appealing to the very pragmatic mind of the runner. It was a concept that did not include as a key component the idea that if one did not agree with the religion, one would be damned to eternal fire and brimstone. The downside of not being in tuned with the various psychological ideas was simply a certain amount of unhappiness and anxiety, a far more palatable consequence. Scientific study and statistical analysis took the place of "mumbo-jumbo" and "faith" without explanation. The runner found this to be a far more appealing explanation of human behavior and the human condition. No delusions, no "faith only" explanations of life and death, no mythology and fairytales, only science and logic. In keeping with that logic and as a natural progression of events, ahead lay mile twenty-two…

chapter twenty-two: the mind

In every race, as in life, there comes a time when one feels intuitively that the end of the task or, in this case, the race is rapidly approaching. At mile twenty-two, with only four miles remaining in the race, the runner had reached that point in this race. He was now very confident that he would complete the marathon running and in reasonably good shape. What now remained in question was at what pace he would run the remaining four miles. Instinctively, he knew that he should remain conservative in his choices; there were still hurdles to overcome. Also, his body, although holding up well, was becoming increasingly weary. He knew that to stop now for any reason, such as relieving himself, would make finishing strongly exceedingly more difficult. In fact, peeing was out of the question! If necessary, he would pee in his shorts rather than stop; the accumulated sweat would prevent anyone from noticing, not that it mattered at this point. Only finishing strong was important. With these thoughts in mind, he strode confidently forward.

"In his mind"...that thought was profound. The Mind: so powerful, so meaningful, so significant in every aspect of life. The Mind: the difference between short life and meaningful old age. The Mind: the determining factor between political fairness and totalitarian madness. The controlling factor between scientific explanations and unexplained "miracles". Very much a reality: the difference between life and death. One person's senility was another person's alert old age; and, in the present situation, the difference between a smooth, satisfying, successful marathon and hitting a "wall". Psychologists and others experts often scoffed at the idea of willpower, but, in a very real sense, with the vast majority of the participants in great shape, it was and is the Mind, "willpower", thought power that determined the difference between success and failure. The Mind: so complex and yet so elementary; but always so essential to all human endeavors. The one factor that seemingly separated humanity from other forms of life. The entity that allowed men to devise all manner of religions and philosophies. The entity that made you smart and me dumb, stupid or "slow". Believe it or not, it was the power of the mind, above all other things, that controlled all aspects, nuances, subtleties, joys, sadnesses, power and powerlessness in life.

As the runner contemplated the impact of the power of the mind, there was no way that he could ignore the tremendous effect that this was having upon himself. The power of the Mind was **everything** in the long, long run…everything! It determined whether one continued or stopped… ran or walked…completed the race or didn't. But more; the Mind determined whether one lived an exciting, thrilling life or one died of monotony; the monotony of foreclosing creativity. Intellectual freedom… belief in experiencing all aspects of life…no holds barred…stretching out and approaching the godhead…in fact, it could be said that the mind was god, and that part of all of us, that spiritual element in all of us, was god as manifested through our minds. Our minds, yours and mine, was that part of the creator in our being; our spirit, our souls, our connection with the universe. God, Allah, Buddha, Nirvana, Zoroaster, along with the many other names of deities, were your Mind. You are god; we are god! Relish it… savor your connection with infinity!

Amidst such thoughts, the reality of the run asserted itself. Amidst the usual water, Gatorade and hoopla, just down the road and around the bend, lay mile twenty-three!

chapter twenty-three: knowledge

Smoothly, with a good feeling, the runner passed the Mile-twenty-three marker. Once again, the subtle aching of having run so many miles permeated the runner's essence; not just his body, not simply his physical entity, but also every other facet of his being. The constant running had penetrated a level unknown to short runners, week-end joggers and even "gym rats". At this moment, the runner had obtained another level of physical awareness. He was running and yet he wasn't. He was so tired that, in a strange way, he was not at all tired. His body was responding to all the months of training. Despite all the trepidation, the internal fear of the idea of running so far, an internal power, an internal essence had taken over. It was as though one foot simply planted itself in front of the other. No pain, no thoughts, only the continuation of the task at hand. It was, indeed, a strange and yet wonderful feeling. Often long distance runners had a feeling of uniqueness; that what they were experiencing was something of which only they were aware. It was a strange feeling, but undeniable. It was as though if you had not run twenty-plus miles, you had no way of knowing what the experience was about. It was an exclusive club which no initiation or entry fee could gain one admittance. Either you had done it or you hadn't; you were in or you weren't. Fortunately, the runner was all the way in!

As with the other miles in such a long run, thoughts drifted. This was a good thing. It shifted one's thoughts from the immediate task, with its incumbent agony to other more pleasant, more cerebral thoughts. As usual, the runner's thoughts drifted…drifted to thoughts of knowledge. Knowledge: a condition universally sought, often claimed but rarely achieved. A goal sought by virtually every meaningful person and society but, likewise, a goal rarely obtained.

The runner liked to think of himself as somewhat knowledgeable but also as a person in an eternal quest for knowledge. Knowledge, unlike wisdom, was a condition, a plateau obtainable to varying degrees by virtually everyone. Knowledge was simply the pursuit of information. Sometimes that information was very meaningful, perhaps, even critical to one pursuit or another. At other times, the information could be seemingly totally frivolous or irrelevant. However, the runner had learned in life that knowledge which appeared to be frivolous often, at some later time, could prove to be extremely relevant. With that in mind, the runner was of the firm belief that all knowledge was important. In that spirit, the runner's pursuit of knowledge of any sort was relentless. It might be the capital of Tanzania, the height of the tallest mountains on the seven continents or, perhaps, some subtle nuance in the local traffic laws. It mattered not to the runner; it was all important. Important also, was the distinction between "knowledge" and other philosophically important ideas, such as "wisdom" and "truth". Knowledge, the runner understood, was not necessarily wisdom; the two did not go hand-in-hand. Although both were of critical importance to the intellectual evolution of humanity, they were distinctly different. Knowledge was information; the compilation and memorization of such. Wisdom, by contrast, was the processing of that knowledge; understanding what knowledge was important to which situations and what knowledge was unconnected or even detrimental to certain conditions. Hitler was knowledgeable, albeit in a certain evil way, while Mahatma Gandhi had knowledge and wisdom. Not only was knowledge not wisdom, but there was also the further danger of one having false knowledge. Even more daunting was the possibility of someone in a position of power disseminating false knowledge. The results of such actions could be and, historically, had been catastrophic, with bad governments controlling the people through the use of evil propaganda. The concept of truth was even more troubling. There were "universal truths", as defined by any number of philosophers, and there was the truth according to "John Doe". That particular version of the truth was simply whatever that particular person deemed it: "telling it like it is". In reality, of course, that concept had, in fact, little or nothing to do with truth. The pursuit of true knowledge should be life long; the truth depended on what philosophy, what religion or what person to which one happened to subscribe.

The friendly sounds of familiar bells, whistles, bands and, generally enthusiastic people began to grow louder. With great happiness and relief, mile twenty-four suddenly appeared. For the runner, that was all the knowledge that he currently needed.

chapter twenty-four: wisdom

Mile 24; 2.2 to go! Less than a 5-k. Just over two miles, something normally easily done. But, of course, in the long race, nothing was easy; nothing to be taken for granted. Always, there lurked danger; danger of some unforeseen calamity. A hidden pothole, a sudden loss of energy, or worse, the will to continue. However, the runner felt confident that none of these things would happen. At this point, come hell or high water, he was going to finish the race, running and strong! The only decision left was to determine at what pace to finish. The runner felt pretty good for someone who had run 24 miles. He was not dragging; his pace was steady. Perhaps, a bit of acceleration was in order. Maybe a little kick for the finish…to finish in style, flying passed stragglers at the finish line with thousands of people watching. Perhaps, if he were lucky, the announcer would look up his bib number and call out his name at the finish line, although, despite hundreds of races, this had never occurred.

Despite these delusions of grandeur, the runner clearly knew that it was too early for a finishing kick. His body, despite the psychological numbness that had set in at this stage of the race, was weary. Too much of a push too soon could still be problematic. He disparately wanted to finish strong, running smoothly to the finish. This called for prudence and patience. Simply hold your pace for the next mile or so and then, with less than a mile to go, kick it in to the finish. At this point in the race the runner knew that certain conditions, of paramount importance earlier in the race, were virtually meaningless now. The weather, for example, no longer mattered. A blizzard could suddenly strike and yet he would finish the race. He knew from his pre-race preparation that there were no large, spirit breaking hills in the last two miles, no unusual terrain with which to content. He knew that he was going to finish in decent shape. It was a good feeling!

With these reassuring thoughts in mind, once again, as was he prone, the runner's mind drifted to other thoughts. He had spent what seemed like much time considering knowledge recently, but he felt as though something was missing from his analysis: wisdom. The runner knew that great knowledge could, and often did exist without the necessary wisdom to effectively utilize that knowledge. Many people, to varying degrees, were knowledgeable: colleges professors, professionals and, simply lay people of limited education who simply liked to read a lot. These people, and many more possessed great knowledge; an immense recall of great masses of trivial information. Almost all of the runner's colleagues in the eminent law school which he had attended, were great intellects possessing great knowledge in many areas. And yet, many of those self same people were not wise. They were very "smart" but they were not "wise". Virtually all of these people, after graduation, would ascend to high level jobs in society in which they would weld considerable influence. In some cases, these very same folks would become the key policy makers for the great nation. Some, in fact, would actually become the leaders of the nation. And yet, despite their great knowledge, many of them would eventually make very unwise decisions, some of which would have a catastrophic effect on the nation and the world. The result of these ill begotten decisions would be the mistreatment and even deaths of millions of people both in the nation and throughout the World. Knowledge without wisdom could be a very dangerous thing. To make matters worse, relatively few people possessed wisdom; and among those who did, even fewer cared to participate in systems politics, with it selfishness, greed, power mongering and corruption. Wisdom was about the unique ability to synthesize knowledge and ideas into meaningful conclusions. Conclusions that included at their core the concepts of selflessness, gratuitousness and humility. The key to wisdom was accepting the idea that the ultimate goal of all knowledge was the greater good of all humanity and, further, the greater good of all beings, whomever or wherever they might be. Wisdom accepted history as a guideline and rejected those policies that had proven ineffective or disastrous in the past. Wisdom was insight. It was the understanding that knowledge without high purpose was often wasted on the petty gains of the few at the expense of the many. That misuse of knowledge, unchecked, would ultimately lead to the demise of humankind. Unfortunately, in the great Nation, rarely did those aforeto mentioned people in positions of power adhere to the universal concepts of wisdom. The results were predictable and unfortunate: worldwide wars, starvation and disease, all preventable and needless. It is, indeed, a sad state of affairs when just, fair and doable policies are scuttled for the momentary power and wealth of a few ruthless people, while the wise sage with the answer to all the world's problems, sits on a mountaintop somewhere totally unheeded. And those who dare to speak out are silenced, incarcerated or assassinated. So sad and yet, apparently, it is the path that we have chosen.

Interesting enough, as the runner approached the 25-mile marker, the raucous merrymakers were at a minimum. There was the last obligatory water station which almost none of the runners used, but little else. Apparently, at this stage in the race, everyone, runners and workers alike, realized that it was all over "but the shouting"! As the runner crossed the 25-mile line, he knew that all he had to do was maintain for less than 1.2 miles, a mere stroll in the park…

chapter twenty-five: contentment

The day remained quite beautiful as the runner began mile 26 of the long run. He smiled internally, knowing now that simply maintaining his current pace would get him to the finish line in under 10 minutes. In fact, a broad grin etched across his face; he actually wanted to laugh out loud in exhilaration at the mere thought of completing yet another marathon. He had run many, perhaps, a dozen or more, however, the feeling of excitement as he neared the finish was always unique. The tingling throughout his body, the light-headedness, the sense of satisfaction never got old. To the contrary, it felt really good! In the words of that old *Queen* song, "Another one bites the dust". He was smokin'!

Approaching the end of the long run, the Runner felt a familiar sense   contentment at his soon to be completed accomplishment. Contentment… a condition in life often spoken of, but seldom achieved. It was, indeed, an elusive mistress. The idea of contentment represented to the Runner an interesting paradox. While almost anybody and everybody would list "contentment" as a goal to be desired in life, those self-same people would be in a quandary to define exactly what was contentment. Though it was and is clearly something more than momentary happiness, and it is apparently some sort of global condition, beyond that definitions become less certain. Contentment in life is a goal for an ultimate state of being in life. While an extremely difficult level to reach, for those who reach that goal, it often appears to be easily obtainable. To others, those who have not achieved that level,   reaching that level seems virtually impossible. First, one must define exactly what contentment encompasses for each individual; is it a religious condition, a psychological state of mind or something else? Is it simply being at peace with one's station in life. Despite this seeming simplicity, true contentment is often difficult to obtain. Most people have adopted societal definitions of "contentment" that, in fact, are not related to true contentment. Money, a desirable partner, material objects or a good meal, while appealing, are not related to true contentment. Being happy with life, one's condition, one's friends and experiencing "peace of mind" in one's life despite life's constant challenges, are the overt manifestations of contentment. Contentment is total happiness! 'Tis a consummation devotedly to be desired."

Ahead, amidst much fanfare and frivolity, with the large banner marked "FINISH" in sight, was the 26-mile marker.

chapter twenty-six: the meaning of life

With the finish line in sight, the Runner was now confident that he would finish the long race running. He continued to feel good, all things considered, and the day continued to be pleasant. His feeling now was that this race was a done deal. At this point he wondered: why? Why had he run the race to begin with; what was the reasoning for running such a long race? Certainly, from a physiological perspective, there was no reason for a human being to run 26 miles. Physiologists had long since determined that a human only needed to run 15 miles a week to get the maximum aerobic benefit. There was, therefore, no physical reason to run a marathon. The benefit from running a marathon was more a philosophical and psychological gain for the runner. It was more akin to reaching a higher level of life; being closer to the godhead; finding true meaning in life.

With that thought, the Runner wondered what, indeed, was the meaning of life. What does "the meaning of life" mean? Is it even important? What was the origin of the idea of the meaning of life? Who cares?

In religious circles, the meaning of life was associated with being righteous and "good". In the case of Christianity, with not being a sinner and understanding one's spirituality. Also, there was the connection to the afterlife and the ultimate connection to a supreme being: to meeting God or

Allah, etc. For highly religious folk, these concepts defined the meaning of life.

From a philosophical perspective, the meaning of life was quite different. The ultimate existential question was; does life have meaning at all? Often, the answer was no, as with Jean Paul Sartre in *Being and Nothingness.* The correct philosophical question then becomes, if life has no meaning, should one, as a purest, commit suicide?

For the Runner, the meaning of life was indelibly tied to the enjoyment and appreciation of life; sort of "I live therefore I am". Life has given one the opportunity to enjoy the wonders of life, therefore, the meaning of life is derived from the appreciation of life. In following, living a meaningful life enhances the meaning of life. Being good to other beings, being selfless, being humble in successes, forthright in one's given profession, being kind to all people, promoting peace on earth and keeping a smile upon your lips and joy in your heart; these things, collectively, represented the true meaning of life. The true meaning of life is the joy of living...

As the Runner crossed the finish line, he was overwhelmed with satisfaction at completing the long run. He was happy: for life, for humanity and for the World. Although this was only one race, one marathon, the meanings derived from the run were deep, almost religious in their magnitude. The long race, itself, was over but life was just beginning. For billions of people throughout the World and for the Runner, the ending of one race was simply the beginning of a great quest; the quest for peace, universal happiness and eternal love.

THE END